Sierra Nevada
BYWAYS

51 of the Sierra Nevada's Best Backcountry Drives

By TONY HUEGEL

 WILDERNESS PRESS • BERKELEY, CA

Sierra Nevada Byways: 51 of the Sierra Nevada's Best Backcountry Drives

1st EDITION 1994
2nd EDITION May 2001
3rd EDITION November 2008

Copyright © 1994, 2001, and 2008 by Tony Huegel

All photos, including cover photos, by the author, except the photos on pp. 15
and 94 © 2008 by Michael Routh, http://sanmiguelphotography.com
Maps: Jerry Painter and Lisa Pletka
Drawings on pp. 13 and 14 by Joey Gifford and copyright © 2008 by Tony Huegel
Index: Sylvia Coates
Cover and interior design and layout: Lisa Pletka
Book editor: Laura Shauger

ISBN 978-0-89997-473-6

Manufactured in China

Published by: **Wilderness Press**
                1345 8th Street
                Berkeley, CA 94710
                (800) 443-7227; FAX (510) 558-1696
                info@wildernesspress.com
                www.wildernesspress.com

Visit our website for a complete listing of our books and for ordering
information.

Cover photo: Coyote Flat Road near Bishop provides views of Middle
                 Palisade Glacier and peaks of the Palisade Group in the
                 John Muir Wilderness (Tour 22).

Gatefold flap: *(top)* Baker Lake, accessed on a foot trail in the John Muir Wil-
                   derness, is a reward of exploring the Coyote Flat area (Tour 22).
                   (middle) An ancient undersea volcano created Sierra Buttes
                   (Tour 1).

Frontispiece: Buttermilk Country (Tour 23) has fantastic views of the Sierra.

SAFETY NOTICE: Although Wilderness Press and the author have made every
attempt to ensure that the information in this book is accurate at press time, they
are not responsible for any loss, damage, injury or inconvenience that may occur
to anyone while using this book. You are responsible for your own safety and
health while in the wild. The fact that a road is described in this book does not
mean that it will be safe for you. Be aware that road conditions can change from
day to day. Always check local conditions and know your own limitations.

Disclaimer

Sierra Nevada Byways has been prepared to help you enjoy backcountry driving. It assumes you will be driving a high-clearance four-wheel-drive vehicle that is properly equipped for backcountry travel on unpaved, sometimes unmaintained and primitive backcountry roads. It is not intended to be an exhaustive, all-encompassing authority on backcountry driving, nor is it intended to be your only source of information about the subject.

There are risks and dangers that are inevitable when driving in the backcountry. The condition of all unpaved backcountry roads can deteriorate quickly and substantially at any time. Thus, you may encounter road conditions considerably worse than what is described here. If you drive the routes listed in this book, or any other backcountry roads, you assume all risks, dangers and liability that may result from your actions. The author and publisher of this book disclaim any and all liability for any injury, loss or damage that you, your passengers or your vehicle may incur.

Exercise the caution and good judgment that visiting the backcountry demands. Bring the proper supplies. Be prepared to deal with inclement weather, accidents, injuries, breakdowns and other problems alone, because help will almost always be far away and a long time coming.

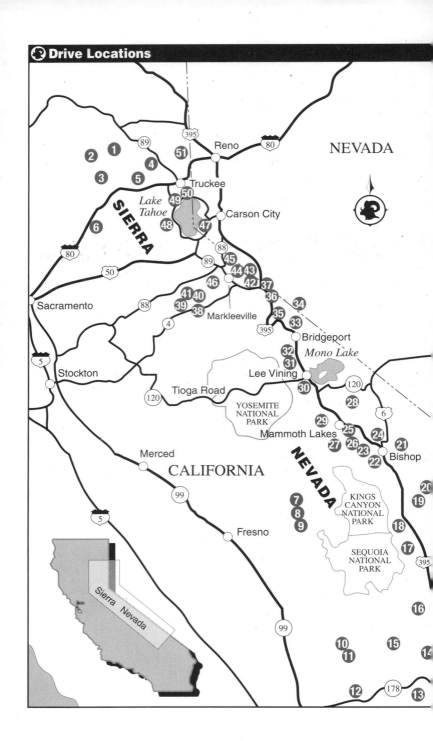

CONTENTS

The Tours

Preface

Hiking. Backpacking. Mountain biking. When I was younger, fitter and more footloose, I enjoyed them all. But life always seems to make more, not fewer, demands on our time. Thus, over the years work, family, lawn care and, I must admit, the passing of my physical prime took me away from those once-cherished modes of backcountry travel. As middle age appeared on the horizon, I worried that my days of wandering the wild were over.

Then I discovered that the West's most beautiful and remote regions, occasionally even wilderness areas where mechanized travel is usually prohibited, are crossed by unpaved, often little-known backcountry roads. I learned that with a factory-stock sport-utility vehicle, equipped with high clearance and four-wheel drive, I could have a wildland experience in comfort and convenience, whether for a few hours or a few days. Bringing whatever amenities I wanted, I could explore rugged mountain ranges, high plateaus and remote desert canyons by day and then, if I didn't want to camp, relax at a motel at night.

I'd broken free of the limitations of time, distance and physical ability. Since many of the West's most rural backroads are relied on by people who live off the land, I found most to be easily drivable, while others were rough enough to provide exhilarating moments of adventure and challenge.

Sierra Nevada Byways, part of my Backcountry Byways series of adventure-driving guidebooks, will take you along many of the most beautiful and historic unpaved roads in the largest and highest mountain range in the Lower 48. You will experience cool forests, verdant meadows, sky-scraping peaks, glacial basins, high-desert valleys and narrow canyons. You will follow the trails of forty-niners and emigrants over remote mountain passes, through deep river valleys and forgotten ghost towns, on roads that range from primitive 4x4 trails to graded dirt and gravel. Whether you want to get away for a few hours, a day, a weekend or longer, the backcountry byways of the Sierra Nevada have just what you're looking for.

Acknowledgments

Many people and organizations helped me produce *Sierra Nevada Byways*. First among them are my wife, Lynn MacAusland, and our two children, Hannah and Land. They accompanied me on many of the drives, and put up with prolonged absences while I researched the rest alone.

I couldn't have produced the book without the help of the U.S. Forest Service and Bureau of Land Management staffers who generously and patiently shared their knowledge. Jerry Painter made an enormous contribution with the maps he produced for all but one route in the second edition. Graphic designer Joey Gifford contributed a map to that edition as well. I am indebted as well to nature photographer Michael Routh of San Miguel Photography (http://sanmiguelphotography.com) for his route suggestions, companionship, enthusiasm and support. He generously contributed several photographs that add considerably to the book's depiction of the eastern Sierra Nevada. I am also grateful to Dimitry Struve, who also suggested routes. The late Ed Dunkley, a recreational four-wheeling pioneer who helped build the California Association of Four Wheel Drive Clubs, contributed his expertise to the two "Diggins'" routes. Bill Sauser was generous with his time and knowledge of the Mammoth Lakes area.

Michael Dobrin, of Michael Dobrin Public Relations in Alameda, California, provided invaluable support and enthusiasm that helped to make my multistate Backcountry Byways series possible. I am grateful as well to Toyota Motor Sales, Inc., for providing the comfortable, capable and unfailingly reliable sport-utility vehicles that I use to research the series, which amounts to the ultimate SUV road test. Over thousands of backcountry miles, I have never had a breakdown in either the Toyota 4Runners I've owned, or the Toyotas I've borrowed.

The cartographic department of the Automobile Club of Southern California has long been helpful by providing copies of their high-quality maps. Benchmark Maps, producer of *California Road & Recreation Atlas,* has generously provided copies for my research. The Post Company of Idaho Falls, Idaho, provided generous support and encouragement early in the book's development. Finally, Wilderness Press of Berkeley, California, has done a great deal over the years to steadily enhance the quality of the series. I still have my 1972 edition of their *Sierra North,* the backpacking guide that introduced me to the Sierra Nevada, one of the greatest places on Earth. Thanks to Roslyn Bullas, Lisa Pletka and Laura Shauger, all of whom put considerable time and effort into this new edition.

A panoramic vista rewards visitors who climb Sierra Buttes' 176 stairs (Tour 1).

The Sierra Nevada Experience
Roaming the Range of Light

Anyone who has waited in line for a wilderness backpacking permit, a ski lift or a chance to climb Mt. Whitney knows the appeal of California's Sierra Nevada. And anyone who's joined or just wondered at the dot-com "gold rush," cheered a 49ers touchdown, eaten Central Valley produce watered by Sierra Nevada runoff or worn a pair of Levi's jeans has experienced the historic, cultural, economic and environmental influence of the Sierra Nevada.

Christened the "Snowy Range" by the Spanish, the Sierra Nevada is the largest and highest single mountain range in the Lower 48, covering almost as much of California as the Alps of France, Switzerland and Italy cover of Europe. While the Rocky and Appalachian mountains are comprised of a number of individual ranges, the Sierra Nevada is one massive, primarily granite, downward-extending block, what geologists call a batholith. Thus, the range is correctly referred to in the singular form, Sierra, not Sierras.

The Sierra Nevada's blue-ribbon peak, 14,495-foot Mt. Whitney, is the highest in the United States outside of Alaska. Yet Whitney is only about 80 miles from Death Valley's Badwater Basin, which, at 232 feet below sea level, is the lowest point in the western hemisphere. Thirteen Sierra Nevada peaks exceed 14,000 feet. Giant sequoias grow more than 300 feet tall. Kings Canyon plunges more than 7,000 feet, deeper than Arizona's Grand Canyon and the Snake River's Hells Canyon. Owens Valley, a Great Basin trough between the Sierra and the White-Inyo Range, lies 10,000 feet below the highest summits that flank it.

Each year, millions of people take advantage of the easy access to this ultimate outdoor playground. The ski slopes of Mammoth Lakes are about six hours from Los Angeles. It's an easy four hours or so from San Francisco's sprawling suburbs to Yosemite Valley, the beleaguered destination of about 4 million people a year. Access to the Sierra's wonders is so easy, and the Sierra's recreational offerings are so diverse, that on holiday weekends the nickname "Range of Light," coined by conservationist John Muir, could be changed to "Range of Headlights."

The Sierra Nevada is some 400 miles long, stretching like a spine from the northwest to southwest, from the confluence with the Cascade Range at the north end to the Tehachapis just north of Los Angeles. For roughly 140 miles of the Sierra's length, between Tioga Road (U.S. 120) through Yosemite National Park in the north to Sherman Pass and Kennedy Meadow roads in the south, no roads cross the Sierra. The range is 50 to 80 miles wide, reaching from some of the world's most productive farmlands in the Central Valley to two great deserts, the Great Basin and the Mojave.

Looking at the Sierra today, it's hard to visualize what was here before: a low, rolling plain beneath a primordial sea. The Sierra emerged through the forces of plate tectonics, the moving, colliding and subducting of plates of the Earth's crust. About 250 million years ago the eastbound, oceanic Pacific Plate and the westbound, continental North American Plate collided. The Pacific Plate dove beneath the North American Plate, in a process called subduction, scraping up sediments, stoking volcanic activity and superheating the subterranean rock. Some 200 million years ago a pool of molten rock and magma, which would eventually become the Sierra Nevada, began to form 10 miles below the surface.

About 80 million years ago, as the magma cooled and rose toward the surface, uplifting began. Overlying ocean-floor sediments 5 to 10 miles thick were folded, twisted and lifted above sea level, and then eroded. Gold-bearing quartz veins formed as the last of the hot granite cooled. Eventually, the predecessor of the Sierra Nevada began to appear as erosion wore the thick sedimentary cap away. (Remnants of this cap, called roof pendants, can be seen on the crest as darkly colored masses of rock on the uppermost portions of peaks. The vertical "tombstone rocks" one sees in the western foothills are seabed remnants.) Erosion carried the sediments from atop the Sierra batholith westward, filling today's Central Valley with material 5,000 to 10,000 feet deep. By about 40 million years ago the Sierra Nevada consisted of low, rolling granitic hills and broad valleys.

By perhaps 30 million years ago the ancestral Sierra had been eroded to a range a few thousand feet high at most. Then the San Andreas Fault shifted, causing a major uplift. About 25 million years ago a period of volcanism began that buried the northern Sierra and filled the lowland valleys. This period of volcanism ended 5 million years ago, and most of the volcanic material has eroded away.

About 10 million to 12 million years ago another period of uplift began. Three million years ago, as the Earth cooled and the first Sierra glaciers formed, it accelerated. The Sierra block was tilted westward. The eastern flank rose higher and more abruptly, leaving the western side with a much more gradual slope. Similar uneven upward pressure lifted the southern segment higher than the northern segment, creating the exceptionally high southern peaks and leaving the lower, northern section sloping downward.

The Sierra Nevada continue to rise, perhaps keeping pace with erosion. The effects of the tectonic collision that gave them birth continue to manifest themselves as well, especially on the eastern side, where the region's obvious and unsettling volcanic and seismic unrest continues.

Today's Sierra would not look as it does without the work of glaciers. From cirques to hanging valleys, long U-shaped canyons and rocky moraines, glaciers left their imprint all over the Sierra. The Sierra have experienced multiple glacial ice ages. The first was 3 million years ago. The heaviest period of glaciation occurred about 60,000 years ago, when an ice cap 275 miles long and 40 miles wide blanketed the Sierra. The most recent, a mini ice age, occurred 600 years ago. The glaciers' most famous work was done in Yosemite Valley and the similar, but now inundated, Hetch Hetchy Valley. The 60 to 70 tiny remnant glaciers that exist in the Sierra today are from the latter, shorter ice age.

Humans have existed in the Sierra Nevada for thousands of years. The stories are told at many locales: the bedrock mortars where Native Americans once ground acorns, the streamside rock piles where forty-niners panned for gold, the passes crossed by pioneers and railroaders, even in the corridor now occupied by Interstate 80, the only interstate across the Sierra.

The discovery of gold in the American River at Sutter's Mill in 1848 spurred one of mankind's greatest and swiftest migrations, an entrepreneurial, multiracial, multiethnic, international rush to get rich in California that has yet to abate. Today, one can hardly imagine American history without that icon of individual initiative, the forty-niner peering hopefully into his pan of fine Sierra gravel.

The saga of the Donner Party was written in the Sierra. Chinese laborers built the most difficult and perilous segment of the world's first transcontinental railroad here. During World War II, thousands of Japanese-Americans

Bygone California remains along bucolic Deer Creek Road (Tour 10).

were interned at the base of the eastern Sierra, at a pear- and apple-growing center called Manzanar in Owens Valley.

What would Los Angeles be today if it hadn't been able to siphon off the waters of Owens Valley, or San Francisco without Hetch Hetchy Reservoir? Would we eat as well or house ourselves as well without the rivers and forests of the western slope? Imagine the California lifestyle without the legendary ability to drive in a few hours from the ocean to Gold Country, from the suburbs of San Bernardino to the ski slopes of Mammoth Mountain, or from Lake Tahoe to Death Valley.

The Sierra Nevada forms a dividing line between two worlds. Driving to the Sierra from the populated coastal areas and across the Central Valley, one finds the gently sloping, well-watered western foothills pastoral, quaint and user-friendly. Life is good west of the crest, with upward of 50 inches of precipitation a year, numerous rivers and lots of roads for those who head for the hills each weekend. Climbing toward the crest, one encounters the Sierra's harder face. The timber grows thick, and granite is everywhere. Over Donner, Carson, Monitor or Ebbetts passes, the traveler plunges down one of the steepest mountain escarpments in the world to be greeted by a vast, high desert that lies in the Sierra's rain shadow.

Pacific air currents, moving from west to east, dump their moisture on the Sierra, making them one of the snowiest places anywhere in winter. By the time the currents reach the eastern side, little moisture is left. So here in the rain shadow, life makes do with 5 to 15 inches of precipitation a year. Relatively few people live here. Most who do hug the base of the range, where the snowmelt runs.

Exploitation of the mountains' natural wealth has taken a heavy toll on both the state's native population and ecology. From the use of powerful hydraulic streams used to mine gold in the 19th century to the massive cutting of giant sequoias, from overcrowding in Yosemite and development in the Lake Tahoe Basin and the draining of Owens Valley by Los Angeles, humans have inflicted heavy blows.

For those who seek outdoor recreation and adventure surrounded by world-class beauty, the Sierra arguably exceeds California's two other defining landscapes, the coast and the deserts. For millions of people, the California coast is largely a visual rather than participatory experience. The deserts—where place names often invoke death and the devil—can inspire trepidation and respect. If we go there at all, we don't stay long. By contrast, the Sierra offers a huge range of year-round activities suited to just about everyone. For a major mountain range, the weather, especially in summer and fall, could hardly be more accommodating. From sightseers, campers, climbers, hikers, water skiers, kayakers, anglers and four-wheelers to history buffs, mountain bikers, photographers and cross-country and downhill skiers, anyone can find fun in the Sierra.

To fully appreciate the region dominated by the Sierra one needs to venture not just into the mountains themselves but also into the deserts and mountains nearby. Just east of the Sierra stand the White Mountains, the Great Basin's highest. Although they rival the Sierra in height, they could hardly be more different. Because they stand in the Sierra's rain shadow, they lack the Sierra's conifer forests, grasslands, lakes and streams. Denied adequate moisture, they never experienced glaciers. Yet the Whites' harsh environment is home to bristlecone pines that are thousands of years old, among the oldest living things on Earth. With roads that climb to well over 11,000 feet, the White Mountains provide a unique high-elevation driving experience through rocky, rolling mountaintops.

South of the Whites, the geologically-linked Inyo Mountains have beautiful canyons, basins and vistas. Even the Sweetwater Mountains, just west of the Nevada line, have soaring peaks, rocky crests and historic mining camps. These neighboring ranges have something in common with the Sierra besides the rain shadow: All three provide stunning big-picture views of the High Sierra and the vast region it influences.

Throughout the Sierra and its neighboring ranges thread hundreds of miles of unpaved, often little-traveled and little-known backcountry roads. The motoring counterparts to hiking trails, they include some of the most scenic and historic backroads anywhere. Many are rudimentary old wagon roads. Some have been used by ranchers for generations. Others are well-maintained, graveled byways. Scratched into mountainsides, over remote passes, through forests, across deserts and subalpine flats, they have been largely overlooked by the motoring public. Yet they provide fascinating and often exhilarating opportunities to explore the Sierra. They take adventurous travelers up canyons carved by glaciers and across desert expanses paved with ancient lava flows. They follow routes taken by emigrants and forty-niners. They wind past remote gold-rush camps and ghost towns, through stands of Joshua trees at the desert's edge, to sky-scraping ridges and along plunging river gorges.

The backcountry driving tours in *Sierra Nevada Byways* will take you far from the crowds, and well off the beaten tourist path. All you have to do is turn the page, and then turn the key.

The rocky little road through Laurel Canyon (Tour 27) leads up a long glacial-carved trough.

Backcountry Touring 101

Sierra Nevada Byways is intended to introduce the adventure of back-country touring to people who travel in factory-stock, high-clearance, four-wheel-drive sport-utility vehicles equipped for possibly rough off-highway conditions. A few of the routes will appeal to more serious four-wheeling enthusiasts, and many are suitable as well for dual-sport motorcycle enthusiasts. Relatively few people who drive stock SUVs, in particular, take advantage of what their vehicles can do, so if that's what you're driving, I'm going to assume that your experience is limited and provide some basic know-how. My hope is to help you have a safe and enjoyable experience while protecting the Sierra's natural environment as well as its historic and cultural sites.

KNOW YOUR VEHICLE Some automakers, eager to tap into the motoring public's yen for at least the visage of ruggedness, have begun to apply the label "sport-utility" to just about anything with wheels. Don't be fooled. Know what you're driving, and drive within the vehicle's limits as well as your own.

Familiarize yourself with your four-wheel-drive system. Is it a full-time, part-time or automatic system? In a full-time, or permanent, 4WD system, all four wheels are continuously engaged as driving wheels; there is no 2WD mode. (A multimode system, however, will include a 2WD mode.) Full-time 4WD uses either a center differential or viscous coupling to allow the front and rear axles to turn independently for typical daily driving. Some systems allow the driver to "lock" the center differential so that, in poor conditions, both axles will turn together for greater traction. Some vehicles, like Toyota's 4Runner, Land Cruiser and FJ Cruiser, can be purchased with driver-engaged locking rear differentials—often called "lockers"—that greatly enhance rear-wheel traction. In many circumstances, particularly if you must crawl over rocks, ledges and deep ruts, a locking differential will vastly improve your ability to get through. It will deliver full power to both driving wheels and eliminate an "open" differential's tendency to transfer power to the wheel with the least traction.

A part-time 4WD system uses only the rear wheels as driving wheels until the driver engages 4WD. A part-time system must be disengaged from 4WD on pavement to avoid excessive drive train stress. An automatic system is designed to sense on its own when 4WD should be engaged. All-wheel-drive (AWD) systems, such as those used in some passenger cars and vans, provide power to all four wheels much as full-time 4WD systems do. Many, though not all, AWD vehicles should be thought of as all-weather vehicles, not all-terrain vehicles.

Does your vehicle have a transfer case with low-range gears? More than any other single feature, a transfer case—which is akin to a second transmis-sion—identifies a vehicle suited to all-terrain travel. It sends power to the front axles as well as to the rear axles, and, acting as an auxiliary transmission, provides a wider range of gear ratios for a wider range of driving conditions. Use high-range 2WD for everyday driving in normal conditions, both on pavement and off. Use high-range 4WD when added traction is helpful or necessary on loose or slick surfaces but conditions are not difficult. Use low-range 4WD in difficult low-speed conditions when maximum traction and power are needed and to keep engine revs high while moving slowly through rough or steep terrain.

Does the vehicle have all-season highway tires or all-terrain tires? Tires take a terrible beating in off-highway conditions, for which the latter are designed.

Find out the location and height of the engine's air intake. This knowledge is important to avoid the devastating consequences of sucking water into the engine through the air intake while fording waterways.

Take a look at the vehicle's undercarriage. It should have steel plates—usually called "skid plates"—protecting vital components like the engine oil pan, transmission, transfer case and fuel tank. Skid plates are essential to helping you avoid the kind of expensive and very inconvenient power train damage that obstacles, particularly roadbed rocks, can inflict while traveling primitive roads.

Knowing these things will give you a better sense of your vehicle's capabilities. "Sport-utility vehicle" used to mean brawny all-terrain, all-purpose passenger trucks like Toyota's Land Cruiser and 4Runner, the vehicles I use exclusively to research my Backcountry Byways travel guides. Despite their upscale appointments and matching price tags, they are built for the rigors of off-highway exploring. But lately, automakers, eager to tap into the motoring public's yen for at least the visage of adventure, have begun to apply the label "sport-utility" to just about anything with wheels that can be given an outdoorsy, active-lifestyle look and all-wheel drive. Don't be fooled. Know what you're driving, and drive within the vehicle's limits as well as your own.

KNOW WHERE YOU'RE GOING As detailed as they are, the maps in this book are general overview maps. It's helpful to bring a good regional map in addition to more detailed maps illustrating the specific area you will be visiting and the route you will be driving.

Each tour description recommends readily available maps for finding your way. Typically I recommend more than one map. AAA maps are good regional maps. Those produced by the Automobile Club of Southern California (ACSC), in particular, are excellent.

I find Benchmark Maps' *California Road & Recreation Atlas*, relevant U.S. Forest Service visitor maps, statewide CD-ROM topographic map sets and, if they're available for your destination, National Geographic/Trails Illustrated maps indispensable. These maps often will include useful information about the area's natural and human history, regulations, campgrounds, picnic areas and historic sites. Forest Service maps differentiate between public and private lands. They may be the best all-purpose maps, although some that are still published are becoming outdated. ACSC maps include the mileage between road junctions, which is helpful for navigation. In some cases, separate maps for adjacent national forests will depict the quality of the same road differently. So when buying national forest maps, be sure they are the latest available. U.S. Geological Survey 7.5-minute maps are unnecessary for driving, but they can be useful for hiking or other activities for which you may need greater detail.

These maps can usually be purchased at Forest Service and U.S. Bureau of Land Management offices, bookstores, information centers and outdoor recreation equipment stores. AAA maps are available at their stores. Be aware that all of these maps are revised and reformatted from time to time, so don't be surprised if the exact map I cite differs from the one you find at your retailer. Whichever maps you bring, go over them before you begin the drive. Become familiar with sights and landmarks to watch for along the way. As you travel, keep track of your progress to avoid missing important turnoffs, places of interest and side trips.

Don't expect to find road signs. The agencies that manage backcountry roads and the wildlands they cross do post signs, but they often don't last long. Vandals, especially the gun-toting kind, often make short work of them. If you reach a point where there are several routes to choose from and none has a sign, it's usually best to follow what appears to be the most heavily used route.

Various companies produce topographic maps on CD-ROM. I've used National Geographic/Trails Illustrated's state sets. If you do a lot of backcountry traveling, CD-ROM map sets are useful indeed for plotting a route, recording Global Positioning System waypoints, checking elevations, and for seeing where you've been if you used a GPS unit to mark waypoints or record a track. An issue to be aware of is the lack of compatibility among CD-ROM maps and GPS units. If you want to download maps between your GPS unit and your computer, you will likely have to use your GPS unit manufacturer's proprietary mapping software.

Global Positioning System units are not necessary, but they are useful. You may more easily find specific locations—places of interest and campsites, for example—if you know their GPS coordinates. You also can record routes and waypoints before you leave home and upload them to the unit for use on your trip. Their tracking features enable you to precisely keep track of where you've been and to find your way back. I use two Garmin GPS units: a small one that I can carry in a pocket while I'm on foot, and another that is mounted on my dashboard for driving.

To identify GPS coordinates, I use the Garmin default datum, position settings and coordinate formats: WGS84 datum, and the "hddd°mm.mmm'" coordinate format to display latitude and longitude in degrees and decimal minutes. Garmin units and some others place the "N" and "W" symbols at the start of latitude and longitude coordinates (they've traditionally been placed at the end of each coordinate in other contexts), so for consistency I also present them in that format. Some GPS coordinates in *Sierra Nevada Byways* were recorded on-site. Most were taken from National Geographic CD-ROM maps using the NAD83/WGS84 datums, and the degrees and decimal minutes coordinate format. Whatever GPS unit and mapping program you choose, you must use the datum and coordinate format in *Sierra Nevada Byways* or you will end up with different positions. Since Backcountry Byways guides are driving guides, not geocaching or bushwhacking guides, you should have no trouble locating the correct roads and junctions.

When venturing into unfamiliar territory, it's sometimes best to rely on road numbers rather than road names. That's because rural and backcountry roads sometimes have more than one name. You may find that roads can have more than one numerical designation as well. Counties, for example, may assign a number that is different from the one assigned by the Forest Service.

As you wander the wild, remember that the settlers, ranchers, miners and loggers who made these roads didn't have your safety in mind.

WEATHER AND WHEN TO GO The Sierra Nevada is the largest and highest mountain range in the Lower 48, and the greater Sierra region has a wide range of climatic zones. These mountains do their part to perpetuate California's sunny image, providing visitors with exceptionally good mountain weather in summer and fall. While visitors to the Colorado Rockies can count on violent summertime thunderstorms, and even road-closing snow by mid-September, travelers in the Sierra can reasonably expect sunny days and even tentless nights.

Depending on elevation, which varies dramatically on these routes, plan on going from early summer through fall and to higher elevations from mid-summer to early fall. The high desert at the foot of the eastern escarpment is hot and dry in summer. The lower foothills also are dry in summer (and fire-prone), and can get darn hot as well. Above, say, 4,500 feet things cool off considerably, especially once you enter the fir and pine forests.

In spring, streams can be swollen with runoff, roads may be muddy and still blocked by snow, and the weather is unsettled. A road that is clear for miles can remain blocked as late as August by a slow-melting, late-season snowdrift lingering in a single spot of shade. As autumn approaches, remember that the days are growing shorter. Begin your adventures early enough to avoid driving these roads after dark.

Since nature has a knack for rudely closing roads without considering our plans, it can be useful to stop at a visitors center or to call ahead. Even then, however, finding out the latest road conditions can be difficult. Visitors centers and ranger stations are often staffed by volunteers who can help with campground locations and such, but may not know the region's backcountry roads very well. The most knowledgeable people at the Forest Service and Bureau of Land Management, which oversee vast expanses of public lands, are often out in the field. Their ability to monitor conditions along remote backcountry roads and trails is limited as well. Often, you will just have to go see for yourself.

GOING ALONE There is security in having more than one vehicle, and more than one source of ideas and labor if things go awry. When you're on vacation, however, or venturing off for a few hours, a day or a weekend, you and yours will probably go alone, in a single vehicle. Now and then, too, a two-track going off to a canyon or mountain range will unexpectedly catch our eye, and you will succumb to its allure. I often do. In fact, I've been exploring the West's wildest roads alone much of the time for many years. Just be sure you're driving a reliable vehicle. (My Toyota 4Runners, including the one that is coming up on 200,000 miles, many of them off-highway miles, have never broken down.)

Be sensible, prepared for trouble and able to handle difficult situations and emergencies alone. That said, during certain seasons, particularly summer, you may be surprised by how popular some of these roads can be. You may well have them to yourself during the work week, but on weekends you'll likely have company. The more remote roads may provide genuine solitude, but you will be sharing others with all sorts of users, from mountain bikers and hikers to all-terrain vehicle riders, motorcyclists, ranchers, loggers and others. Be alert, and be considerate.

RULES OF THE ROAD Even in places where no one will be watching, there are rules to follow, and practices that help to preserve natural and historic areas. The intent behind them is simple: to keep you safe, to keep your vehicle operating reliably, and to protect fragile wildlands and cultural sites from abusive and destructive activities. Misconduct and mistakes can result in personal injury, damage to your vehicle, areas being closed and perhaps even legal penalties.

Here are some things to keep in mind:

- Your vehicle must be street-legal to take these drives. Obey traffic laws and regulatory signs, wear your seat belt, and keep the kids buckled up.

- Drive only on established roads where motor vehicles are permitted. Mechanized travel of any kind, including motorcycles and mountain bikes, is not allowed in designated wilderness areas and wilderness study areas unless a legal corridor exists. Never go "off-road," make a new route, or follow the tracks of someone who did.

- Avoid steep hillsides, stream banks and boggy areas.

- If you get lost or stuck, stay with your vehicle unless you are certain help is nearby. A vehicle will be much easier for searchers to find than you will be if you're out there wandering aimlessly.

- Do not disturb archaeological or historic sites or artifacts. They are not replaceable, and may be protected from theft and vandalism by federal laws. Do not touch Native American rock art. Treat historic structures like the irreplaceable relics of bygone times that they are.

- Do not use archaeological or historic sites for picnics or camping unless they are developed for those purposes. The more time people spend at them, the more they are degraded.

- Some of the places you will visit remain marred by old, perhaps even dangerous mines. View them from a distance.

- Blind curves are common. Round them carefully.

- If you camp, use minimum-impact practices and leave no trace of your stay. Camp only at established campsites or areas that show previous use. Bring your own water (many developed campgrounds are dry due to changed water-quality standards), and camp at least 300 feet from the banks of streams, ponds and lakes to avoid damage and pollution, and to allow access by wildlife. Clean up the campsite before you leave, and take your trash and wastes with you. Bring your own firewood.

- Leave gates as you find them, i.e., open or closed. Don't disturb live-stock.

- Don't drink directly from streams, which can be contaminated by that longtime bane of backpackers, the parasite giardia, and other organisms and contaminants.

- Avoid parking on grass, because hot exhaust systems can ignite fires.

GO PREPARED Things can and will go wrong out there, so be prepared to handle problems alone, perhaps even to spend a night or two outside. On the supplies side, the basics of backcountry driving are already on the packing list of experienced outdoor enthusiasts: maps, compass, extra eyeglasses and keys, a good first-aid kit, binoculars, trash bags, matches, clothing for inclement weather, hats and sunscreen, insect repellent, blankets or sleeping bags, flashlights or headlamps and extra batteries, plenty of food and water (a gallon per person per day is considered the absolute minimum) and something that will make you easy to spot should someone come looking for you. Don't forget to augment your supplies with enough nonperishable food and water for a couple of days in case you get stranded.

Here's a basic checklist of more auto-oriented things to bring:

- A topped-off fuel tank. My rule is to fill up before every backcountry drive. You will use your vehicle's low gears much of the time, which will mean higher fuel consumption than during on-highway driving. It shouldn't be necessary to carry extra fuel on any of these drives; I rarely do. If you do, strap the container to the exterior of the vehicle, preferably the roof. Keep the container full so that dangerous fumes won't build up inside.

- A personal locator device. These small, portable units are much like GPS units. In fact, they use the Global Positioning System to send emergency alerts. In the past, they cost hundreds of dollars and were to be used only in life-threatening situations. However, a more affordable device, SPOT satellite personal messenger, has come onto the market. It can send "OK" messages transmitting your location via GPS coordinates and Google Maps, and signaling that all's well and you're just checking in; a "Help" message with GPS coordinates for your location in situations that are not life-threatening; and a 911 alert signal to dispatch emergency responders to your exact location. After years of adventuring alone, and having plenty of misadventures, I've purchased a SPOT. At the very least, it provides peace of mind.

- A shovel. Mine has been a lifesaver and is the most useful tool I carry. Yours will be, too.

- Good all-terrain tires, a good (and properly inflated) spare and jack, a small board to support the jack on dirt, a couple of cans of pressurized tire sealant (available at auto parts and department stores), a small electric air compressor (the kind that plugs into a vehicle cigarette lighter, also available at department stores), a tire pressure gauge and tire chains. Be careful in old mine sites and ghost towns—they are often littered with old, rusty nails.

- Some basic tools include a folding saw (for removing deadfall), jumper cables, duct tape, electrical tape, baling wire, spare fuses, a multipurpose knife, a high-strength tow strap, a fire extinguisher and a plastic sheet or tarp to put on the ground. An assortment of screws, washers, nuts and such could come in handy as well, especially if you're driving an older or modified (meaning trouble-prone) vehicle.

- Sometimes I bring my mountain bike as a backup vehicle. Since I do a lot of exploring, I also use it to check out places that I don't want to drive to. On rough terrain, when the vehicle can pitch suddenly and hard from side to side, many roof-mounted bike racks won't keep a bike securely in place. I once had a bike break loose and come crashing down. Since then, however, I've been using Yakima's heavy-duty SprocketRocket, which has worked well in the wild.

- A portable toilet. This can consist of an inexpensive five-gallon plastic utility bucket, a seat lid and a box of WAG BAGs or other brand disposable and biodegradable waste bags made for the purpose. The bags contain a gelling agent and decay catalyst so the waste-filled bags can be disposed of in landfills through standard garbage-disposal methods. All of these items are available at outdoor-recreation supply stores. This is less and less an optional item because increasing numbers of people are accessing the same backcountry areas. Nobody likes to encounter the waste of others, and natural ecosystems can only handle so much. I believe strongly that these should be on the packing list of everyone who ventures, even for a day, into wildlands where sanitation facilities are not available. Some areas managed by the National Park Service now require these types of systems, at minimum.

- Campfire permit from the local U.S. Forest Service office. Persistent drought and extreme wildfire danger in the West, including the Sierra

Nevada, mean that campfires may be banned outside of developed campgrounds at the time of your trip.

I keep much of my gear ready to go in large plastic storage containers. It's also important to secure your cargo so that it doesn't get tossed about on rough terrain.

Cellular telephones and lighter-powered chargers can be handy, too, although I've found that they often don't work in the wild. Satellite phones can be rented at increasingly affordable rates, if you really need to stay in touch. My experience with them, however, hasn't inspired great confidence in their ability to transmit reliably.

OFF-HIGHWAY DRIVING Driving more slowly and cautiously than you do on paved roads will get you where you want to go and back again most of the time. Here are some tips for those inevitable times when the going will get rough:

All thumbs? You won't be for long if you forget to keep them on the outside of the steering wheel. Otherwise, the wheel's spokes can badly injure your thumbs if a front wheel is suddenly jerked in an unexpected direction. If the steering wheel is being rocked back and forth by the terrain, keep your hands loose on the wheel, at 10 and 2 o'clock, and your thumbs on the outside of the wheel.

Leaning forward in especially rough conditions and keeping your back away from the seat back will help prevent you from being tossed about so much.

Uphill traffic has the right of way. If practical, it is usually easier and safer to back up to a pullout, using gravity as a brake, than to back down a slope while fighting the pull of gravity. There may well be times, however, when it just makes sense to let the downhill vehicle have the right of way.

Think ahead. If you have a part-time 4WD system, engage it before you need it to stay out of trouble.

When in doubt, scout. If you're unsure or uneasy about the way forward, check it out on foot first.

Air down in sand, deep mud and rocky terrain. While standard tire pressure usually will suffice, sand may require temporarily airing down (letting air out) to 15 psi or perhaps even 10 psi to expand the tire's "footprint," or contact patch, for greater flotation and traction. On rocky terrain, airing down will soften the ride and lessen the punishment the roadbed inflicts on the suspension. On especially rocky and steep terrain, airing down also will allow the tires to conform to the rocks so they can grip better. Shallow mud can be underlain by firm ground, so normal tire inflation or even overinflation can help tires penetrate to terra firma.

Tire manufacturer Dunlop recommends deflating tires in off-highway conditions by the following percentages from normal pressure:

Deflating tires improves traction.

- Rough terrain: -10 percent
- Sand: -25 to -40 percent
- Mud: -30 percent
- Loose ground at very low speed for short distances: as much as -50 percent

The risk in airing down is that you will lose ground clearance and the tires' thin sidewalls will bulge, making them more vulnerable to cuts and punctures. Remember to air the tires up to their proper pressure before driving at speed or on pavement, using a small electric air compressor if necessary. (I bring a small cylinder of compressed CO_2, which can be refilled at welding supply centers, and an air hose long enough to reach each wheel.)

Maintain speed and forward momentum in sand, mud and snow. The general recommendation is to go as slow as you can, but as fast as you must. Stopping can be the worst thing to do. Higher gears tend to be more effective in poor-traction conditions than lower gears. Because of the range of problems that driving in mud poses (severe roadbed damage, vehicle damage and transporting biological organisms from one ecosystem to another), avoid it if you can. If you begin to lose traction in mud, turn the steering wheel rapidly one way and then the other, back and forth. If you do get stuck, dig out the sides of the tires to relieve suction. Then pack debris around the tires for traction.

Dust storms and flash floods are dangerous. Blinding dust storms can kick up suddenly in the desert. Do not attempt to drive through one. Instead, pull over to a safe place, turn off the engine to avoid clogging the air filter, and wait it out, keeping windows and doors closed. In spring, and during and after summer storms, you are likely to encounter flooded roads in the desert. Check the depth and speed of the water before fording. If it's fast and deep, stay out.

Stick to the high points. When the going gets particularly rough, shift into low range, go slow and steady, and keep the tires on the high spots, thus keeping the undercarriage high and away from obstacles that can damage the differentials or other components. Let the tires roll over the rocks. Do not let large rocks pass directly beneath the vehicle.

Straddle ruts. Let them pass beneath the vehicle. If you must cross a rut, do so at an angle, easing one tire at a time across it. Do the same for depressions, dips, ledges or "steps," and ditches.

If you get stuck, don't panic. Calmly analyze the situation. With thought and work, you will get out. In soft surfaces, don't spin the tires, which will only dig you in deeper. Raise the vehicle with a good jack and fill in the space beneath and around the affected wheels with dirt and debris until you've created a slight ramp (it can help to make it high enough so that the wheel's on a downhill slope, facing the direction you want to go in).

Straddle ruts.

If your vehicle gets high-centered, that is, the undercarriage is hung up atop an obstacle like a rock, jack it up and see if the obstacle can be removed. Or build small ramps, using dirt and rocks, beneath the tires so you can drive off the obstacle.

To get over a ledge, either use the rock ramp that is likely to be there already or build one from a few nearby rocks. You may need to put one wheel over at a time.

Cross ruts at an angle, one wheel at a time.

A word about earth-moving: If you've had to build a rudimentary ramp to get over an obstacle or out of a rut, afterward put the dirt and rocks back where you found them. Don't leave an excavation site behind.

Be prepared to remove dead-fall from the roadway. Occasionally you may encounter a fallen tree or limb in the road. It's usually possible to drive around it. If you must drive over it, approach it at an angle and put one wheel over it at a time. If you carry a folding saw, as I do, cut it away. If the obstacle is too large to cut or move by hand, consider using your tow strap to pull it out of the way.

It can help to have a spotter on particularly rough terrain, such as Wheeler Ridge Road (Tour 26).

Have someone act as a spotter. This will help you maneuver through difficult places. Use low range and a low gear for better control and to keep the engine revs up.

Try not to spin your tires, which can tear up the road and get you stuck, or stuck worse than you may already be. Some new SUVs have sophisticated four-wheel electronic traction-control systems that are intended to eliminate wheel spin by instantly transferring power from spinning wheels to the wheel or wheels with traction. A few, particularly some Toyotas, can be purchased with locking differentials. These mechanisms vastly improve your ability to get through or out of nasty off-highway situations by equalizing power to the driving wheels and eliminating the differential's tendency to transfer power to the wheel with the least traction. I recommend them. If you encounter a hill that is badly chewed by the spinning of tires of vehicles that lack locking differentials or traction-control systems, shift into low range and keep your wheels on the high spots between the holes.

Be careful when climbing a steep, blind hilltop. Before climbing over it, learn what's up there and on the other side. Depending on how steep it is and how much power your vehicle has, shift into low range and first or second gear. Drive straight up, accelerate as you climb, keep moving, then slow down as you near the top.

If the engine stalls on a hill, stop and immediately set the parking brake hard and tight. Here, an automatic transmission can help you get going again easily. Just shift into "park" and turn the key. If you have a manual transmission and are facing downhill, you may be able to compression-start the engine. If you're facing uphill, try shifting into low-range first gear. Turn the engine over without clutching, and let the starter motor move things along a bit until the engine starts and takes over. Otherwise, you'll have to work the clutch, hand brake and accelerator simultaneously to get going again without rolling backward. Modern clutch-equipped vehicles require the driver to depress the clutch pedal to start the engine, which is fine in a parking lot but difficult on a steep mountain incline. However, some SUVs have clutch bypass switches that let you start the engine without depressing the clutch, a great help when stalled on a climb.

If you can't make it up a hill, don't try to turn around. Stop, and put the transmission in low-range reverse. Tilt the exterior mirrors, if you can, so that you can see what the rear tires are doing. Then slowly back straight down. Never descend in neutral, relying on the brakes. If you must apply the brakes, do so lightly and steadily to avoid losing traction and going into a slide. Go straight down steep inclines, using low range and the lowest driving gear so the engine can help brake. But remember that automatic transmissions, which I think are best overall, don't provide as much engine-braking ability as manual transmissions.

Avoid traversing the side of a steep hill. Occasionally, though, mountain roads do cross slopes, sometimes tilting the vehicle "off-camber," or toward the downhill side. It's an unnerving

Cross streams slowly, and watch for rocks.

experience, especially if the road has become wet and perhaps a bit slick. Lean heavily (no pun intended) toward caution under such circumstances. You might want to remove cargo from the roof to lower your vehicle's already-high center of gravity. Then go slowly. It might help to turn the front wheels into the hill. If you decide not to continue, do not attempt to turn around. Tilt the exterior mirrors so you can watch the rear tires, shift into low-range reverse for greater low-speed control, and slowly back up until you reach a spot where you can turn around safely.

Avoid crossing waterways if you can. Fording streams and shallow rivers is fun, to be sure. But many living things reside in or otherwise depend on streams, and can be harmed by careless and unnecessary crossings that stir up sediment and erode stream banks. If you must cross, use an established crossing point. Check with a stick if you're unsure of its depth, comparing the depth to your vehicle. Or walk across first. Don't cross if the current is fast and deep. Never enter a desert wash if it's flooding. Check for deep holes. Often, a somewhat fast-moving perennial stream will be safer to cross than a sluggish one, because continuously moving water prevents sediments from settling, keeping the bed rocky and firm. Slow-moving or still water, on the other hand, lets sediment and mud build up.

A slow, steady crossing will stir up less sediment and make less of a bow wake, thus minimizing stream bank erosion and the impact on plants and wildlife. (In particularly deep water, however, a bow wake can create a beneficial air pocket for the engine.)

Be aware of where your engine's air intake is. It may not be high enough to ford deep water. If it isn't, it could suck water into the engine, causing severe damage.

In deep crossings, it's also possible for water to be drawn into your vehicle's gear boxes unless the differential vents have been raised to a point that will keep them above the water. To avoid that, I've extended my 4Runner's front and rear differential vents up into the engine compartment. I removed the vent caps, slipped hoses onto the vent extensions, secured them with hose clamps, threaded long sections of hose through the undercarriage into the engine compartment, then inserted new differential vents into the ends of the hoses, again secured with hose clamps. Extending the vents also helps to keep them clear of dust and dirt, which can clog them, causing pressure to build up inside the differentials and forcing oil out through the seals. I try to avoid water that is higher than the wheel hubs.

Once across, stop and inspect the vehicle. The brakes will be wet, so use them a few times to dry them out. The tires will also be wet and may not grip the roadbed as well.

SUVs AND ACCESSORIES Properly equipped sport-utility vehicles are built to take people to places that sedans, vans and station wagons either cannot go, or shouldn't. Despite their comforts, they are rugged and reliable transport—backcountry or frontcountry. They can go from the showroom straight into the hills without modifications.

One of my family's two Toyota 4Runners has a five-speed manual transmission and a stock four-cylinder engine, which I've found to be adequate even when it's loaded with the four of us and our camping gear. The other has a relatively fuel-frugal V6 and automatic transmission. I've never felt any need for a large, thirsty V8.

Manual transmissions have advantages. They can be more responsive, tend to provide slightly better fuel mileage and are better at engine braking on steep terrain. Many clutch-equipped vehicles require the driver to fully depress the clutch pedal when starting the engine, which can be a problem if you're stalled on a steep hill. However, on a steep incline you can shift the transmission into low-range first gear and let the starter motor start the engine while it simultaneously pulls the vehicle forward. It's also possible to compression-start the engine if the starter or battery dies.

I prefer automatic transmissions. I find them easier to use when the going is rough, where having a manual transmission can require three feet: one for the brake, one for the clutch and one for the accelerator, all working pretty much simultaneously.

I've learned to appreciate options that I once dismissed as unnecessary. Easily adjusted electric side mirrors, for example, will pay for themselves the first time you have to back up a narrow shelf road with a killer drop-off. When I'm exploring narrow, high-walled canyons, a sunroof is a handy option indeed.

There is a huge four-wheel-drive accessories market. Are those add-ons necessary? It depends on how much, and what type of, adventure motoring you plan to do. The requirements of serious four-wheeling on technically challenging routes differ from those of backcountry touring. The former can require extensive vehicle modifications, which can degrade on-highway performance and reliability. The latter does not. Still, if you enjoy traveling the West's vast network of backcountry roads, there can be real benefits to adding extra lights, beefier tires, a more versatile roof carrier, heavier skid plates and perhaps even an after-market locking differential to your SUV. (In case you're wondering, I've never owned a winch.)

VEHICLE MAINTENANCE Vehicle maintenance is essential. Backcountry roads are hard on all vehicles, so follow the recommendations in your owner's manual for dusty, wet and muddy conditions. Check the tires often. If you pass through an old mining area, expect to pick up a nail now and then. Always travel with at least one good spare. You will eventually need it.

Wash your vehicle when you return to town to prevent rust and corrosion. You also don't want to carry home the mud, dirt and debris that has collected underneath, because transporting spores, insects and other organisms to disparate geographic regions via off-highway vehicles can spread pests and diseases.

HAVE FUN! Backcountry roads provide terrific opportunities to explore the Sierra Nevada easily and conveniently. And as you travel, tell me what you've found, whether they are mistakes or trips and tips you'd like to see added to future editions. You can visit my Web site at www.backcountrybyways.com or write to me in care of Wilderness Press at info@wildernesspress.com.

Using *Sierra Nevada Byways*

LOCATION Where the drive is.

HIGHLIGHTS An overview of the drive's appealing elements. (The icons accompanying each route suggest additional attractions and activities, such as wildlife, scenery, hiking and biking trails, and campsites or campgrounds.)

DIFFICULTY This is subjective and changeable. Opinions and levels of experience differ. Conditions change as well. I assume you are not a serious four-wheeling enthusiast, that you are traveling in a stock, high-clearance four-wheel-drive (4WD) vehicle with all-terrain tires and a transfer case with high and low range. That said, the ratings are I use are: *easy,* which means the road is maintained and probably won't require 4WD unless conditions deteriorate; *moderate,* which means slower going using 4WD much of the time, with rough spots, possible stream fords, deep ruts, etc., but little or no technical terrain; and *difficult,* which means at least some technical four-wheeling, rough and slow going in low-range 4WD, and the possibility of some vehicle damage. Most routes are rated *easy* and *moderate.*

TIME & DISTANCE The approximate time required to complete the drive, which can vary at your discretion, and the distance you will travel.

MAPS Each description is accompanied by an overview map, with the route highlighted in color. Scale is approximate. For route-finding and greater detail, use at least one of the maps that I cite. Since most of the drives are located in or near national forests, I usually recommend the U.S. Forest Service (USFS) visitor map produced for the national forest where the route is located. I also cite Benchmark Maps' *California Road & Recreation Atlas (CRRA),* and specific maps produced by AAA affiliates Automobile Club of Southern California (ACSC) and the California State Automobile Association (CSAA). In a few routes, I cite particular quadrangles from the U.S. Geological Survey's 7.5-minute series. Maps are revised and redrawn from time to time, so a map I recommend may change between my own updates. At the time of this revision, ACSC was in the process of replacing its county maps with regional maps, so you may have to acquire the regional replacement if a county map is noted and no longer available. Map pages and grid coordinates are cited to make it easier to locate the routes. Sometimes I cite a supplementary brochure that can be useful. You can obtain the maps and brochures from outdoor recreation supply stores, book and map retailers, AAA travel stores and Forest Service offices. Maps are revised and reformatted over time, so it's possible that a map I recommend will no longer be the current one.

INFORMATION An agency that may have details about current road conditions and other information. Telephone numbers, addresses and Web sites (current at the time of publication) are listed in the appendices.

GETTING THERE How to reach the starting point. I typically describe routes going in a particular direction.

REST STOPS Viewpoints, picnic spots, campgrounds, historic sites and such.

THE DRIVE In this section I provide details of the drive, such as descriptions of what you will see, directions, historical background and points of interest. I provide odometer readings to help you stay on track and GPS coordinates using the WGS84 datum, and the degrees and decimal minutes coordinate format (see page 9) for important junctions and points of interest.

Map Symbols

Point of interest	■	Information	?
Paved road	———	Hiking trail	- - - - - -
Easy dirt road	~~~~	Forest or county road	3S01
Primitive road	~ ~ = = ~	Interstate highway	5
Camping	▲	U.S. highway	101
Lake	⬬	State highway	1
Waterway	~~~~	North indicator	↓
Mountain	⌒⌒		
Ranger station	⚑		
Picnic area	⊼		
City or town	○		

Tour Road Types

Paved road	~~~
Easy dirt road	~~~~
Primitive road	~ ~ = = ~

Guide to Tour Highlight Icons

📷 **Photo opportunities**

🚲 **Mountain biking**

🏚 **Historic sites**

⛺ **Camping**

🎣 **Fishing**

🦎 **Rock art**

🚶 **Hiking**

⊼ **Picnicking**

Author's Favorites

Diggins I (Tour 2) and Diggins II (Tour 3)

Forty-niners and later 19th-century argonauts who sifted the gravels of the Sierra's streams, washed away entire mountainsides and bored into the rock searching for gold left a legacy that is still visible in the region of the northern mines. These tours take you to the rugged mountains and remote canyons, gullies and streams where, not only gravel was washed away in the search for riches, but many golden dreams as well.

Jawbone to Lake Isabella (Tour 13)

This southern Sierra tour is fascinating, not only for the terrific scenery, but also because it crosses multiple life zones, from the pale canyons and washes of the Mojave Desert to Joshua tree woodlands, stands of oak and conifer forest.

The Narrows and Papoose Flat (Tour 20)

One way to get an overall view of the Sierra Nevada is to drive high into a neighboring range from which you can view the Sierra. This drive into the Inyo Mountains, which stand east of the Sierra, provides superlative views of the Sierra and lets you experience the drying effect of the Sierra's rain shadow. It won't take more than a few minutes to discover that, from their deep canyons to their rocky flats and lofty peaks, the Inyo Mountains are themselves a spectacular and rewarding destination. The massive granite boulders at Papoose Flat are reminiscent of the eastern Sierra's Alabama Hills, and the walls of The Narrows are a unique sight.

Coyote Flat and Coyote Ridge (Tour 22)

This tour has it all, from views of the high-desert Owens Valley to subalpine basins and lofty ridges below some of the Sierra's highest and most spectacular peaks. The scenery ranks among the best the Sierra has to offer.

Wheeler Ridge Road (Tour 26)

This exhilarating adventure in the eastern Sierra will satisfy those seeking a high-elevation four-wheeling experience. With care, it can be done in a stock SUV equipped with a transfer case, skid plates and high ground clearance. It will reward you with one of the most breathtaking vistas of the Sierra, Owens Valley and the White Mountains that you'll find anywhere.

Boulder Flat (Tour 34) and Jackass Flat (Tour 35)

The Sweetwater Mountains, like the Inyos and the Whites, rise east of the Sierra. As with those other ranges, they are in many ways (publicity and crowds included) eclipsed by the Sierra. The Sweetwaters also provide outstanding views of the alpine spine of their dominant neighbor, but they are an impressive mountain range in their own right, with magnificent peaks, high ridges, multihued basins and historic sites.

The effects of 19th-century hydraulic mining can be seen at Malakoff Diggins State Historic Park (Tour 3).

The

Tours

Sierra Buttes Loop

LOCATION North of State Route 49 at Sierra City, Tahoe National Forest. Sierra County.

HIGHLIGHTS This 4WD adventure includes a mountainside shelf road and awesome views of the historic North Yuba River Valley and northern Sierra. The tour is capped with 360-degree views from the lookout atop 8,587-foot Sierra Buttes **[N39°35.622' W120°38.491']**, which consist of rock that spewed from an undersea volcano 350 million years ago.

DIFFICULTY Easy to moderate. The first 4.7 miles are a narrow shelf road. To reach the buttes, you will drive up a steep 4WD road to a parking area. From there you must hike uphill for a mile or so, then climb 176 stairs to the lookout.

TIME & DISTANCE With the hike to the lookout, it's about 4.5 hours and 16.5 miles for the entire loop from Sierra City to Sierra Buttes, then down to Bassetts, on S.R. 49. (It's about 2 hours and 6.8 miles from Sierra City to the parking area below the lookout.) Allow about 50 minutes for the uphill hike to the lookout, on a rocky 4WD road that is closed to motor vehicles.

MAPS *CRRA* p. 60 (F–G, 5–6). USFS's *Lakes Basin, Sierra Buttes and Plumas-Eureka State Park* (D–F, 5–6). USGS's 7.5-minute *Sierra City*.

INFORMATION Tahoe National Forest, Downieville Ranger District.

GETTING THERE In Sierra City (on S.R. 49), turn north onto Butte Street. Follow it a short distance to a Y junction, at Sierra Buttes Road **[N39°34.018' W120°38.127']**. Go left, and follow the signs for Buttes Lookout and the garbage disposal site. About a mile from town is a gate. The pavement ends here. The route, Forest Service Road 93-2 (Sierra County Road S520), makes a hard right **[N39°34.012' W120°39.150']**.

REST STOPS Sierra City and Bassetts have food and fuel, and there are campgrounds in the area. Visit the nearby Kentucky Mine Museum, east of Sierra City.

THE DRIVE From pavement's end, continue climbing above the valley of the North Yuba River. The mountainside road is rocky and loose, and in some places the brush extends into the roadway. Now and then you will get glimpses of craggy Sierra Buttes. At mile 3.6, pull over to the left and walk out to a knoll overlooking the valley. An even better view is at mile 4.7 **[N39°35.042' W120°40.519']** where a small road branches to the left (west), ending in 0.2 mile at Blue Point, where there is a terrific vista across northern Sierra valleys, canyons and foothills. At mile 0.1 from the Blue Point spur, just around the bend to the right (east), a small, signed, but unnumbered road branches into the trees on the right **[N39°35.282' W120°40.079']**. (This road isn't shown on the USFS maps.) Take it. In 0.4 mile it brings you to the Sierra Buttes 4WD road (93-23), again on the right **[N39°35.282' W120°40.079']**. (After visiting the buttes, take the road ahead down past Packer Lake to Bassetts.) Shift into low range, and climb 1.1 miles to the parking area. Hike up to the lookout **[N39°35.617' W120°38.839']** for one of the Sierra's most impressive vistas. Near the top you'll see names and dates from the late 1800s carved into a large rock. Backtrack down the 4WD trail, and drive down to Bassetts **[N39°37.007' W120°35.534']** on graveled and paved roads.

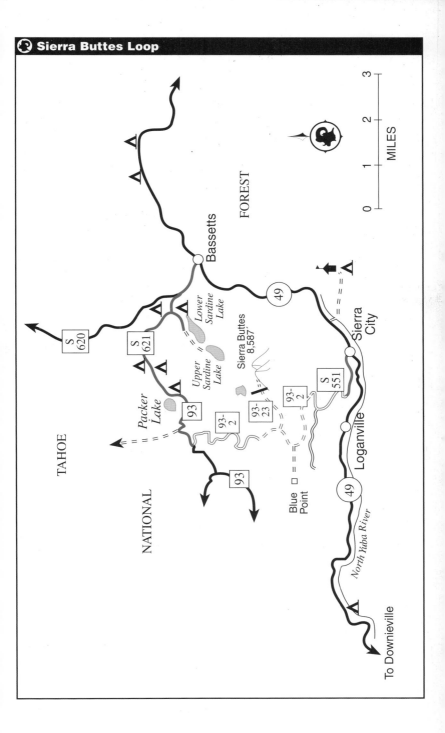

TAHOE

NATIONAL

FOREST

Bassetts

S 620

S 621

Lower Sardine Lake

Upper Sardine Lake

Packer Lake

Sierra Buttes 8,587'

93

93-2

93-23

93-2

S 551

Sierra City

Loganville

Blue Point

North Yuba River

To Downieville

MILES

0 1 2 3

Diggins I

LOCATION Tahoe and Plumas National Forests, between Downieville at the south end and La Porte at the north end. Sierra County.

HIGHLIGHTS This tour takes you through the rugged northern gold country, where mountains were scarred by hydraulic mining. Sights include old mining sites, historic buildings and gold camps from the mid-1800s to 1884. The northern Sierra vista from the lookout atop 6,690-foot Saddleback Mountain is outstanding. You can link up with Diggins II (Tour 3). The gold rush town of Downieville is worth a visit as well.

DIFFICULTY Easy to moderate. Four-wheel-drive Poker Flat Road (Road 800) is steep and can be muddy. Do not ford Canyon Creek during high water. These roads can be closed by storms.

TIME & DISTANCE 3 hours; 29 miles.

MAPS *CRRA* p. 60 (F–G, 3–4). *Tahoe National Forest* (B–C, 3–4) or *Plumas National Forest* (G–H, 6–7).

INFORMATION Plumas National Forest, Feather River Ranger District; Tahoe National Forest, Downieville Ranger District.

GETTING THERE To go north (the way described below): Take State Route 49 to Cannon Point, an overlook above the North Yuba River west of Downieville where there is indeed an old cannon on display. On the north side of the highway is Saddleback Road (509) **[N39°33.476' W120°50.038']** Turn here, and zero your odometer.

To go south: From La Porte, take paved Quincy-La Porte Road (511) northeast for almost a mile, then turn right (east) onto unpaved St. Louis Road (512).

REST STOPS Refer to your map for area campgrounds. There are primitive campsites at Poker Flat, Howland Flat and Yankee Hill. The Saddleback Mountain Lookout **[N39°38.192' W120°51.865']** is a great place to stop.

THE DRIVE At Cannon Point you can gaze into the valley of the North Yuba River. Below is Downieville, named for Scottish prospector Major William Downie whose party of miners was among the first to find gold here in 1849. Saddleback Road (509) climbs on a shelf above the valley, then bends north. At a junction at mile 7.7 **[N39°37.807' W120°51.808']** from S.R. 49, keep to the right and continue ahead, toward Saddleback Lookout and Poker Flat. Another 0.4 mile farther, the spur to the lookout branches right (east) **[N39°38.012' W120°52.058']**. This rough road provides more views of craggy Sierra Buttes (Tour 1), and ends in 0.6 mile.

Continuing toward Poker Flat **[N39°41.587' W120°50.837']**, the road passes Mt. Alma and Democrat Peak, and in a few miles it descends steeply to the ford at Canyon Creek **[N39°41.597' W120°50.719']**. Near Poker Flat, go left at the Y junction, and continue through diggings, sites of early gold mining that remain disturbed. Cross the creek to reach Poker Flat, at the junction of Saddleback and Poker Flat roads **[N39°41.669' W120°50.612']**. Poker Flat was once the hub of a rich gold district where hydraulic mining occurred from the early 1850s to 1884.

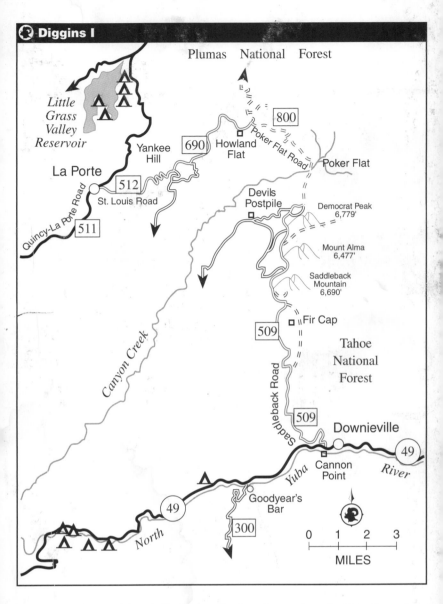

Plumas National Forest

Little Grass Valley Reservoir

La Porte

Yankee Hill

Howland Flat

Poker Flat Road

Poker Flat

Devils Postpile

Democrat Peak 6,779'

Mount Alma 6,477'

Saddleback Mountain 6,690'

Fir Cap

Tahoe National Forest

Downieville

Cannon Point

Goodyear's Bar

Yuba River

North

Canyon Creek

Saddleback Road

St. Louis Road

Quincy-La Porte Road

0 1 2 3 MILES

Poker Flat Road (800) climbs steeply, then descends to the site of Potosi **[N39°42.939' W120°52.460']**. Go left (west) at the fork **[N39°43.015' W120°52.752']** and follow Road 690 to Howland Flat **[N39°42.901' W120°53.147']**. As you approach Howland Flat there is a cemetery amid the trees on the left (south) side of the road **[N39°42.916' W120°52.934']**. The road crosses land that was devastated by hydraulic mining. About 4.8 miles from Howland Flat, take the road that descends to the right **[N39°41.678' W120°55.849']**, toward Yankee Hill. On St. Louis Road, you will pass a bridge built in 1913, then reach pavement east of La Porte **[N39°41.226' W120°58.847']**.

Saddleback Mountain provides a sweeping view of the northern Sierra.

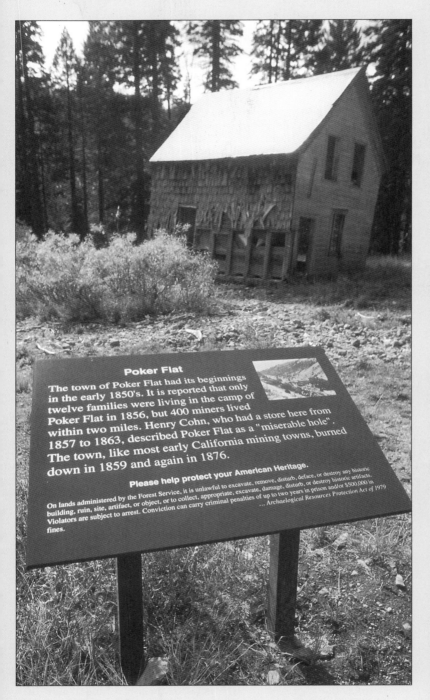

Poker Flat

The town of Poker Flat had its beginnings in the early 1850's. It is reported that only twelve families were living in the camp of Poker Flat in 1856, but 400 miners lived within two miles. Henry Cohn, who had a store here from 1857 to 1863, described Poker Flat as a "miserable hole". The town, like most early California mining towns, burned down in 1859 and again in 1876.

Please help protect your American Heritage.

On lands administered by the Forest Service, it is unlawful to excavate, remove, disturb, deface, or destroy any historic building, ruin, site, artifact, or object, or to collect, appropriate, excavate, damage, disturb, or destroy historic artifacts. Violators are subject to arrest. Conviction can carry criminal penalties of up to two years in prison and/or $500,000 in fines.

... *Archaelogical Resources Protection Act of 1979*

Author Bret Harte (1836–1902) featured gold rush–era Poker Flat in his tale "The Outcasts of Poker Flat."

Diggins II

LOCATION Between Goodyear's Bar (on State Route 49) at the north end, and Nevada City (also on S.R. 49) at the south end. Sierra County.

HIGHLIGHTS This tour combines rugged, forested northern Sierra scenery with 19th-century historic sites like Nevada City, Malakoff Diggins State Historic Park, North Bloomfield, Alleghany, Forest City and Goodyear's Bar, all early North Yuba River mining camps.

DIFFICULTY Easy overall, but rocky and narrow in places. Storms and slides can close the roads north of the Middle Yuba River.

TIME & DISTANCE 3.5 hours; 48 miles.

MAPS *CRRA* pp. 60 (G–H, 3–4) and 65 (A–B, 11–12). *Tahoe National Forest* (C–E, 2–4).

INFORMATION Tahoe National Forest, Downieville and Nevada City ranger districts. Malakoff Diggins State Historic Park.

GETTING THERE **From Nevada City (as described below):** Take State Route 20, then go west on S.R. 49. Soon you'll see the Forest Service office, where you can check road conditions. Just west of it, turn north onto North Bloomfield Road (522) **[N39°16.493' W121°01.285']**. Zero your odometer.

From Goodyear's Bar: About 4 miles west of Downieville on S.R. 49, turn south onto Goodyear Creek Road; cross the river on the old bridge, then follow Mountain House Road (S300) south.

REST STOPS Nevada City and Downieville have services. There are campgrounds at the South Yuba River and Malakoff Diggins. North Bloomfield has restrooms, a picnic area and cabins.

THE DRIVE Paved, narrow and serpentine North Bloomfield Road forks a half mile from the highway **[N39°16.493' W121°01.285']**. Bear right, toward North Bloomfield. At mile 6 it enters the South Yuba River Recreation Area and descends to a bridge over the South Yuba River **[N39°19.807' W120°59.050']**. Pavement ends here.

Climb out of the gorge, then go right at mile 8.7 **[N39°20.479' W120°58.556']**, continuing toward North Bloomfield. At mile 11.2, at Lake City Road, bear right again **[N39°21.543' W120°56.524']**. When you reach mile 11.3 the road enters the park. Here you can view Malakoff Mine, where hillsides were hosed away. A lawsuit ended hydraulic mining in 1884.

Soon you reach picturesque old North Bloomfield **[N39°22.083' W120°54.006']**, once Malakoff's supply center. Note your odometer, and continue north from North Bloomfield on North Bloomfield-Graniteville Road (522). About 1.3 miles from North Bloomfield, bear right on Graniteville Road. About 3.7 miles from North Bloomfield is a junction **[N39°23.728' W120°51.469']**; go right (east), toward Graniteville, for a half mile, then turn left (north) at another junction **[N39°23.716' W120°50.942']** and note your odometer. In about 1.5 miles the road bends to the left (southwest). At about mile 1.6 **[N39°24.675' W120°50.908']** you must take a hard, easy-to-miss turn to the right (north) onto a small road, Moore's Flat Road, and continue past Moore's (a.k.a. Moores) Flat **[N39°25.097' W120°51.149']** and Buck's (a.k.a. Buck) Ranch **[N39°25.663' W120°50.150']**. Note your odometer reading at Buck's Ranch. About 0.8 mile from Buck's Ranch the road (833) bends right **[N39°25.552' W120°49.382']**, but your route is the 4x4

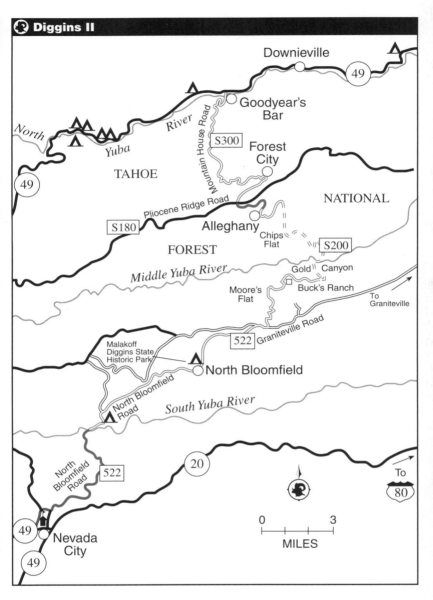

trail ahead that plunges into Gold Canyon **[N39°26.372' W120°48.819']** on the Middle Yuba River. A mile farther, at a junction **[N39°25.587' W120°48.591']**, keep left. Angle right when you reach the river, crossing rock to reach a bridge.

Beyond the river is a sign indicating whether the road ahead is open. (It's often left in the "closed" position regardless of conditions.) Road S200 climbs, bends south then north, and arrives at a junction on Lafayette Ridge **[N39°27.282' W120°50.233']**. Go north through Chips Flat **[N39°27.587' W120°50.104']**. The road crosses another bridge. Go left at a Y junction; continue to Alleghany and Pliocene Ridge Road (S180). Cross the latter, and take Mountain House Road (S300) north **[N39°28.279' W120°52.428']** to historic Forest City and S.R. 49 (10 miles) **[N39°32.531' W120°53.139']**.

Henness Pass Road

LOCATION Between Verdi, Nevada, and California State Route 49, Tahoe National Forest. The east end is in Toiyabe National Forest. Sierra County.

HIGHLIGHTS This historic east-west road over Henness Pass, said to be the only trans-Sierra backcountry road, originally provided an easier alternative into California than that followed by the ill-fated Donner Party of 1846. It is named for Patrick Henness, who developed the pass in 1849 or 1850. With the discovery of the Comstock Lode in 1859 at Virginia City, Nevada, it became the main route between there and Marysville. Declining mine production and the completion of the Transcontinental Railroad in 1869, however, reduced use to local traffic. Near the west end, at the confluence of Oregon Creek and the Middle Yuba, drive through the Oregon Creek covered bridge (circa 1862). East of Camptonville is Sleighville House, a gold rush-era stage stop. Side trips go to the old mining towns of Forest City and Alleghany. West of Jackson Meadow Reservoir the road follows a ridge between the North and Middle Yuba rivers, providing excellent views, particularly of Sierra Buttes (Tour 1). At Kyburz Flat there are some Native American rock-art sites and interpretive signs that explain the area's 2,000-year human history. At the east end, drive up 8,444-foot Verdi Peak for a grand vista. The route is a good mountain-biking opportunity as well.

DIFFICULTY Easy, on asphalt, gravel, dirt and rock. Although remote in places, it's pretty much a high-clearance 2WD road.

TIME & DISTANCE 6 hours and 90 miles with the 13.7-mile (round-trip) spur to Verdi Peak. It can be taken in segments.

MAPS *CRRA* pp. 60–61 (G–H, 2–10). *Tahoe National Forest* (C–D, 2–11). CSAA's *Feather River and Yuba Regions.*

INFORMATION Downieville and Sierraville Ranger Districts, Tahoe National Forest. The brochure *A Historic Driving Tour of the Henness Pass Road* explains 22 sites beginning at S.R. 49.

GETTING THERE To go east: Take S.R. 49 north from Nevada City to the Oregon Creek bridge, then to Camptonville. There, follow Cleveland Avenue east uphill to Henness Pass Road **[N39°27.259' W121°02.731']**.

   To go west: Take Interstate 80 to Verdi, Nevada. Take Bridge Street to Dog Valley/Henness Pass Road. Take Dog Valley/Henness Pass Road to a Y junction, at the turnoff to Dog Valley via Long Valley Road. At the Y junction, Henness Pass Road (860) is the left branch.

REST STOPS Oregon Creek Day Use Area. See the map for campgrounds. Kyburz Flat has toilets and an interpretive trail.

THE DRIVE From Camptonville, take graveled Road 293 along a ridge to Mountain House Road (S300) **[N39°30.007' W120°52.394']**. There, you can detour to historic Forest City and Alleghany, then backtrack to Road S302, a dirt leg of Henness Pass Road, or take the paved segment (Pliocene Ridge Road) east to the dirt portion. This ridgecrest segment (S301), west of Jackson Meadow Reservoir, is the rough-

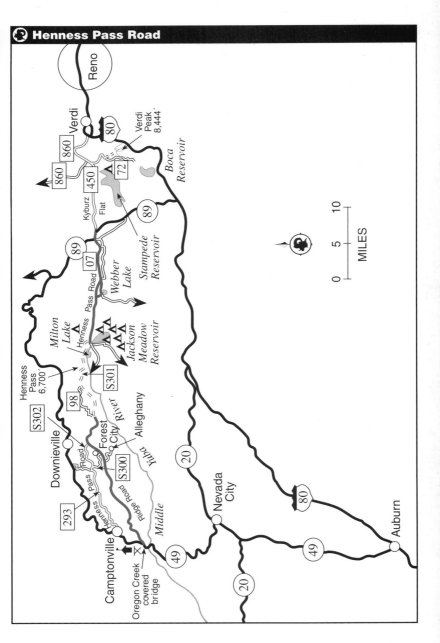

est part. It's also where you cross the pass **[N39°30.027' W120°26.312']**. It joins paved Henness Pass Road (07) at the lake's northwestern corner **[N39°30.564' W120°33.218']**. East of Webber Lake, where the Webber Lake Hotel was built in 1860, and west of State Route 89, the route makes a short detour to the south bank of Little Truckee River.

Grouse Ridge
and Bowman Lake

LOCATION Between State Route 49 and Interstate 80, north of Yuba Gap, Tahoe National Forest.

HIGHLIGHTS This drive winds through a spectacular landscape that includes numerous lakes, high cliffs, canyons, a historic town site and cemetery, an awesome 360-degree vista from the 7,707-foot-high Grouse Ridge Lookout (built in 1923), and mountain biking, hiking, canoeing, fishing and camping opportunities. All of it lies within easy reach of Reno, Sacramento and the Bay Area.

DIFFICULTY The first 10.2 miles of Bowman Lake Road are paved. The unpaved roads are easy but a bit rough.

TIME & DISTANCE There's so much to see that this works best as a two-day camping trip. Plan on driving upward of 70 miles, including 5.3-mile (one-way) Grouse Ridge Road, or even more, depending on which of the side roads you explore.

MAPS *CRRA* pp. 66 (A–B, 2–3) and 60–61 (G–H, 5–7). *Tahoe National Forest* (D–E, 5–7). CSAA's *Feather River and Yuba Regions.*

INFORMATION Nevada City and Sierraville ranger districts, Tahoe National Forest.

GETTING THERE Take U.S. 20 southwest for about 3.7 miles from its junction with I-80 at Yuba Gap (Yuba Pass on some maps). Turn north onto Bowman Lake Road (18) **[N39°18.238' W120°40.289']**. Zero your odometer.

REST STOPS There are developed campgrounds in the area, as well as many primitive campsites. Refer to your map.

THE DRIVE From U.S. 20, Bowman Lake Road (18) winds north through forest and soon crosses the South Fork of the Yuba River at Lang Crossing **[N39°19.136' W120°39.422']**. Then it climbs through a granite canyon to bring you to the Grouse Ridge Road (14) turnoff **[N39°22.203' W120°40.542']** 6.3 miles from the highway. Turn right (east) through the gate, and follow Grouse Ridge Road to a campground **[N39°23.320' W120°36.644']**, the sparkling lakes of Grouse Lakes Basin, and a fire lookout that provides an inspiring vista of the northern Sierra and beyond.

  Bowman Lake **[N39°27.103' W120°39.132']** is about 9 miles north of the Grouse Ridge Road turnoff. At its western end is Bowman House, owned by the Nevada Irrigation District. Cross the bridge over Canyon Creek, and soon you will come to Meadow Lake Road (843) **[N39°27.100' W120°39.268']**. Turn right (east). Meadow Lake Road goes more or less east along the northern edge of Bowman Lake to pretty Meadow Lake and the site of once-bustling Summit City **[N39°24.596' W120°30.172']**. Founded in 1862 by H. W. Hartley, it had 5,000 people in 1864. But the gold that sparked the boom proved too difficult to extract, and the city soon died. Hartley's resting place is well-marked in the old cemetery.

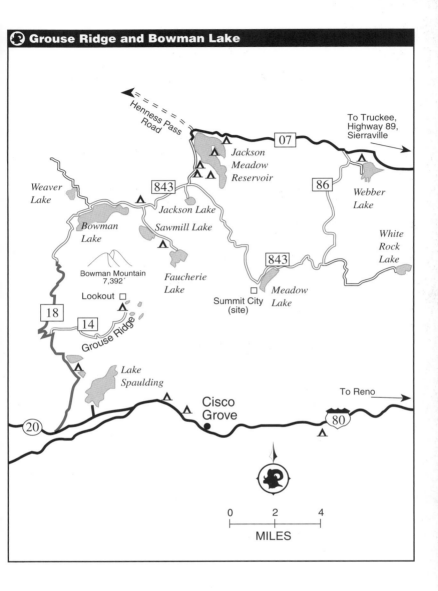

East of the lake turn left (north) on Road 86 **[N39°25.341' W120°26.941']** toward Webber Lake and paved Henness Pass Road (Tour 4; shown as Fiberboard Road on the CSAA map) **[N39°29.989' W120°26.135']**. The latter takes you 9 miles east to State Route 89 **[N39°26.784' W120°12.873']**. (The 10-mile round-trip spur to White Rock Lake, which is nice but can be buggy, may not be worthwhile if your time is limited.)

Kyburz Flat Interpretive Area along gold rush-era Henness Pass Road (Tour 4) explains the area's history and prehistory.

Massive granite ramparts rise above Bowman Lake (Tour 5).

Iowa Hill Loop

LOCATION   On the North Fork of the American River east of Colfax and Interstate 80. Placer County.

HIGHLIGHTS   You edge along beautiful canyons and mountainsides that are still recovering from 19th-century hydraulic gold mining, and cross the North Fork of the American River on a rare single-lane suspension bridge built in 1930.

DIFFICULTY   Easy, though narrow and serpentine. Iowa Hill Road and a mile of Yankee Jim's Road are paved.

TIME & DISTANCE   1.5 hours; 24 miles.

MAPS   *CRRA* p. 65 (C–D, 11–12). *Tahoe National Forest* (G, 3–4). CSAA's *Feather River and Yuba Regions.*

INFORMATION   Placer County.

GETTING THERE   This loop begins and ends at I-80. The route described below starts at Colfax. Exit I-80 at Colfax/State Route 174. On the east side of the interstate (which is going north and south here), take Canyon Way south from the overpass for 0.3 mile. Turn left onto Iowa Hill Road **[N39°05.473' W120°57.047']**. Zero your odometer.

   To go the opposite way, starting farther south on I-80, take the Auburn Street exit to Canyon Way. Take Canyon Way south for 0.7 mile. Turn left onto Yankee Jim's Road.

REST STOPS   Mineral Bar campground, at the river on Iowa Hill Road. There's river access and a toilet at the Colfax-Foresthill Bridge.

THE DRIVE   It didn't take long for the "easy" gold to be taken from the Sierra's rivers and streams during the California gold rush. To extract the gold that lay inside the mountains, in ancient riverbed gravels and sediments, mining companies used high-pressure streams of water to wash away entire mountainsides. You can still see eroded hydraulic mining sites in places like the Iowa Hill district, around the bygone town of the same name. Gold was discovered here in 1853. Three years later weekly production was estimated at $100,000. By 1880, the district had produced $20 million in gold.

   From I-80, Iowa Hill Road plunges into the canyon of the North Fork of the American River, where there's an old suspension bridge that is now just a footbridge. Then the narrow road climbs to Iowa Hill Divide, at mile 8.6. You can see hydraulic mining sites on either side. A bit farther is the site of the town of Iowa Hill **[N39°06.499' W120°51.585']**, destroyed several times by fire. Stop here and take a look at the remains of a vault that once stood inside a Wells Fargo Express Office. (The town of Yankee Jim's stood west of Foresthill, on Yankee Jim's Road.) Follow the signs for Yankee Jim's, Foresthill and Shirttail Canyon. Keep right at a junction at mile 11.2 **[N39°05.575' W120°51.464']**, and follow unpaved Shirttail Canyon Road down into Shirttail Canyon (named for a miner who worked only in a shirt). This enchanting, winding road brings you to Yankee Jim's Road, at mile 17.6 **[N39°02.429' W120°53.157']**. Turn right beyond an old mine adit and waterfall.

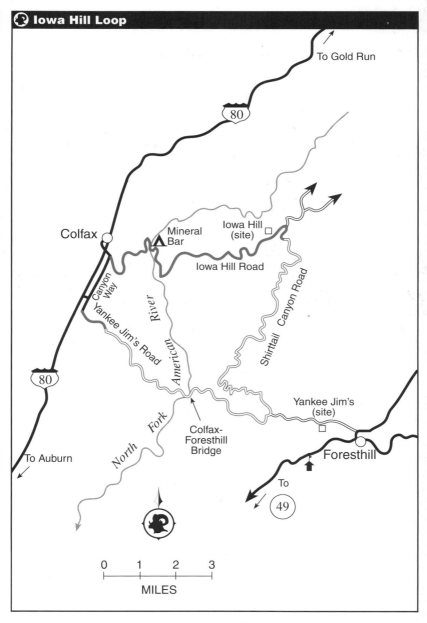

To Gold Run

80

Colfax

Mineral
Bar

Iowa Hill
(site)

Iowa Hill Road

Canyon
Way

Yankee Jim's Road

River

American

North Fork

80

To Auburn

Colfax-
Foresthill
Bridge

Shirttail Canyon Road

Yankee Jim's
(site)

Foresthill

To

49

0   1   2   3

MILES

Soon you reach the old Colfax-Foresthill Bridge **[N39°02.416' W120°54.164']** across the North Fork of the American River, beyond which are more adits, evidence of the drift mining that came after hydraulic mining was banned in 1884. From there you climb again, reaching pavement in 3.6 miles, and Canyon Way 1.1 miles farther **[N39°04.103' W120°57.345']**. You reach I-80 soon thereafter.

Blue Canyon and Ross Crossing

LOCATION   East of Fresno. Sierra National Forest, between Pine Flat and Wishon reservoirs. Fresno County.

HIGHLIGHTS   This long loop takes you along Blue Canyon, through mixed forest of pine and oak, to pretty Haslett Basin and on through granite-strewn Sierra scenery. High points, including Fence Meadow Lookout, provide terrific vistas if the smog isn't too bad.

DIFFICULTY   Easy but long, on a mix of unpaved and marginally paved segments. The Dinkey-Trimmer Road (10S69) is closed from December 12 to May 20 for wildlife protection.

TIME & DISTANCE   3.5–4 hours; 57.4 miles.

MAPS   *CRRA* p. 78 (F–G, 3–4). *Sierra National Forest* (G–H, 6–7).

INFORMATION   Sierra National Forest, Pine Ridge Ranger District.

GETTING THERE   Take State Route 168 northeast to Shaver Lake. Drive east on Dinkey Creek Road. About 9 miles east of Shaver Lake (and about 3 miles west of Dinkey Creek), turn south onto Providence Creek Road **[N37°04.095' W119°10.869']**, Forest Service Road 9. Zero your odometer.

REST STOPS   There are developed and undeveloped campsites along the way, as well as numerous places to stop for a break. Gas, food and lodging are available at Dinkey Creek.

THE DRIVE   Providence Creek Road descends through forest to Blue Canyon and the junction with Big Creek Road **[N37°02.546' W119°14.191']**. Turn left (south), following Big Creek Road (still F.S. Road 9) past the signed turn for Bretz Mill campground, at about mile 9.2. By about mile 13.5 the crude asphalt road surface ends, and the road narrows to a ledge and descends into pretty Haslett Basin. Here, at about mile 15.2, is the junction with Dinkey–Trimmer Road **[N36°58.163' W119°13.000']**. You can go south to reach Pine Flat Reservoir in about 8 miles, and then on to State Route 168 and Fresno. This tour continues winding south on Dinkey–Trimmer Road (10S69), so note your odometer reading and turn left (east) at the junction.

A short distance from the junction, in a picturesque open area, the road crosses Nutmeg Creek on a rustic one-lane bridge. Then it climbs out of the basin, providing outstanding vistas to the south and west. At about mile 20.2 **[N36°56.065' W119°12.231']** is a gate that is closed from December 1 to April 20. (The gate across Road 11S02, to the southeast to Balch Camp, is closed from December 1 to April 1.) The serpentine road bends north now, and mile 25.1 should find you at the turnoff (Road 11S08) **[N36°58.350' W119°10.704']** to Fence Meadow Lookout, which provides a typical panoramic view. Note your odometer again. The road to the lookout is closed from 6 PM to 9:30 AM by a locked gate.

Mile 32.8 brings you to the junction at Nutmeg Saddle **[N36°59.646' W119°10.426']**. The tour goes right, onto Road 10S67 to Road 10S24, Ross Crossing Road.

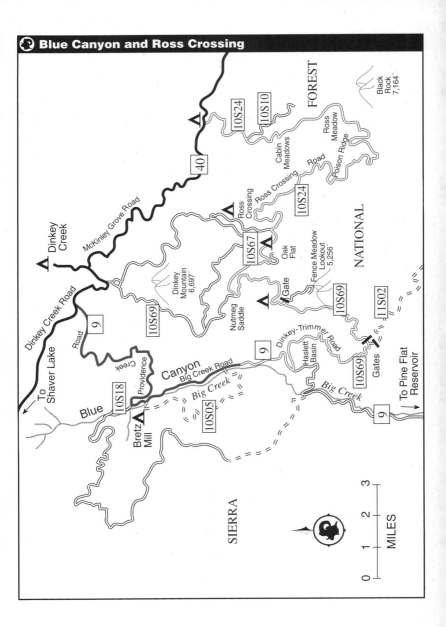

This narrow road descends to another intersection in 4.3 miles **[N36° 58.738'W119°08.068']**; keep right, on Ross Crossing Road. It winds down into another deep canyon and crosses Dinkey Creek on a bridge at Ross Crossing **[N36°59.329' W119°07.469']**, a gorgeous place to stop, have lunch or camp. From here the road climbs again, entering an open area with exposed granite, including the dome of Black Rock. Farther on lies Ross Meadow. The drive continues north to end at mile 57.4 or so, at paved McKinley Grove Road (40) **[N37°00.508' W119°04.293']**, about 9 miles southeast of Dinkey Creek.

Black Rock Road

LOCATION East of Fresno, between Wishon and Pine Flat reservoirs. Sierra National Forest. Fresno County.

HIGHLIGHTS This is a spectacular drive on a narrow shelf road carved into the canyon of the North Fork of the Kings River. The alternate segment above Granite Gorge is particularly impressive. Though it's an easy drive (more than half of this route is paved), you will edge along sheer drop-offs on one-lane segments that cross tiny bridges in two places. There are many vista points and a number of huge Pacific Gas & Electric penstocks, dams and other power-generating facilities.

DIFFICULTY Easy, though narrow and serpentine. The Granite Gorge alternate is moderate.

TIME & DISTANCE 2.5 hours; about 28.5 miles.

MAP *CRRA* p. 78 (F–G, 4–5). *Sierra National Forest* (G–J, 6–7).

INFORMATION Sierra National Forest, Pine Ridge and Kings River Ranger Districts.

GETTING THERE From the Fresno area, make your way east on Trimmer Springs Road to the eastern end of Pine Flat Reservoir. Turn north across the South Fork of the Kings River **[N36°52.282' W119°07.853']**, toward the town of Balch Camp. Zero your odometer.

REST STOPS There are developed campgrounds and other recreation facilities along the South Fork of the Kings River, at Black Rock and Wishon reservoirs, and at Sawmill Flat.

THE DRIVE The paved road takes you through Balch Camp **[N36°54.288' W119°07.363']**, then angles east to climb higher into the mountains, the source of the water that runs the hydroelectric plants here. About 0.4 mile from Balch Camp, the road passes beneath the Dinkey Creek siphon. A couple of miles farther, as you hug the canyon wall high above the North Fork of the Kings River, you cross the first of two hair-raising one-lane bridges. Beyond them the little road passes beneath the Balch Penstocks.

Eventually you reach the turnoff for PG&E's Black Rock Reservoir and campground **[N36°54.884' W119°02.425']**, named for a 7,164-foot peak to the north. The pavement on this winding road ends in another 1.6 miles, at the gated turnoff to the Haas Powerhouse, but the unpaved segment ahead is maintained and easily driven. Beyond that, however, is a particularly narrow segment, and more stunning views of the gorge below. A few miles farther on, high above fantastic Granite Gorge and just before you reach Sawmill Flat campground **[N36°58.171' W119°01.014']**, the road forks **[N36°57.928' W119°00.682']**. The main road, 11S12, continues for 3.5 miles to paved McKinley Grove Road (Forest Service Road 40) **[N36°59.725' W119°01.336']**. I recommend taking the right branch, Road 11S01, a spectacular, moderate shelf road at the head of Granite Gorge that crosses a saddle, passes a small lake, winds through the forest and, 4.5 miles from the turnoff, delivers you to Wishon Reservoir. You'll love it.

To Courtwright
Reservoir

To Dinkey
Creek

*Wishon
Reservoir*

SIERRA

Road

McKinley

Grove

40

11S01

NATIONAL

Gate

11S12

Granite Gorge

Sawmill
Flat

FOREST

River

11S12

Black Rock
7,164´

Patterson Bluffs

Black Rock Road

Gate

*Black Rock
Reservoir*

Black

Balch
Camp

Fork

Kings

North

To Fresno

*Pine Flat
Reservoir*

Kings River Road

Kings River

12S01

To Davis Flat and
Delilah Lookout
(See Tour 9)

0   1   2   3

MILES

Hydroelectric plants generate power along North Fork Kings River, below Wishon Reservoir.

Travelers on Black Rock Road encounter bridges.

Delilah Lookout to Kings River

LOCATION East of Fresno, between Black Oak Flat (State Route 180) and the South Fork of the Kings River. Sequoia National Forest. Fresno County.

HIGHLIGHTS None of the sweeping vistas across the southern Sierra along this drive come close to the panorama at Delilah Lookout **[N36°48.250' W119°07.051']**, which stands atop 5,156-foot Delilah Mountain. (The lookout is a terrific destination by itself.) The northern segment parallels the beautiful South Fork of the Kings River.

DIFFICULTY Easy.

TIME & DISTANCE 3.5 hours; about 30 miles, including the 12-mile side trip to Delilah Lookout.

MAPS *CRRA* pp. 78 (G–H, 4) and 85 (A, 11–12). *Sequoia National Forest* (B–C, 1–3). CSAA's *Sierra Nevada-Yosemite Area* (O–P, 9–10).

INFORMATION Sequoia National Forest, Hume Lake Ranger District.

GETTING THERE From Fresno, take S.R. 180 east into Sequoia National Forest. At Black Oak Flat **[N36°44.848' W119°03.094']**, turn left (northeast) onto Millwood Road/Forest Service Road 12S01 at the sign for Delilah Lookout. Zero your odometer.

REST STOPS There are three developed campgrounds, an undeveloped campground and a picnic area at the north end, along the river. Delilah Lookout is a great place to stop.

THE DRIVE From S.R. 180, take paved Millwood Road (Forest Service Road 12S01) northwest about 2.9 miles to the intersection with Road 12S19 **[N36°46.086' W119°04.454']**, which continues west on Pine Ridge and then northwest. (Road 12S01, which you will return to, continues west and then north from this junction). Note your odometer reading here. Eventually 12S19 bends northwest and passes through a residential area. The ridgeline road provides numerous inspiring vistas of the Central Valley to the north and west and deep canyons to the east.

When you reach a fork almost 3 miles from the junction of 12S01 and 12S19, take the left branch, which is Road 13S75 **[N36°46.922' W119°06.639']**. Note your odometer reading here. In almost 1.8 miles, the main road drops to the left, but there is a branch on the right that goes a short distance to Delilah Lookout and makes a small loop around its base. This has been a fire detection site since 1916, although the current tower dates only to the 1960s.

After visiting the lookout (only operational during periods of high fire danger) return to 13S75, and backtrack to the junction of 12S01 and 12S19. Follow winding, rocky and possibly rutted road 12S01 (Crabtree Road) north. It climbs to Goat Saddle **[N36°48.042' W119°05.341']**, then snakes along a ledge as it descends among rugged and steep canyons to Davis Flat, where it follows Davis Creek through the site of Crabtree **[N36°50.581' W119°05.439']**. The road bends west when it reaches the Kings River at Mill Flat campground

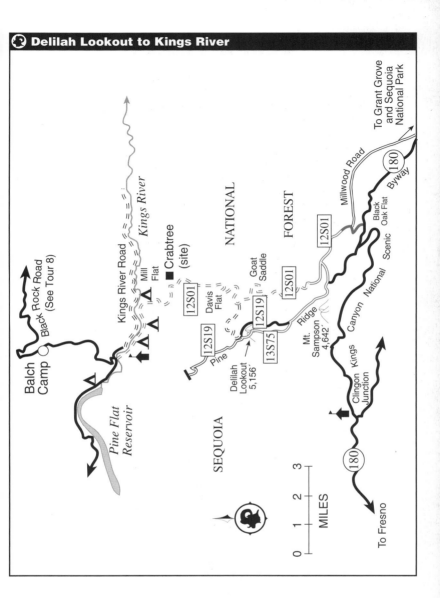

[N36°51.404' W119°05.841']. Soon you come to a steel bridge across the river, which is the end of the drive **[N36°52.241' W119°07.854']**.

From the bridge you can continue west to Pine Flat Reservoir. For more adventure, cross the river and take scenic but dead-end Kings River Road along the north bank. Or take terrific Black Rock Road (Tour 8) along the dramatic canyon of the North Fork of the Kings River in Sierra National Forest.

Deer Creek Drive

LOCATION Tulare County, southeast of Porterville.

HIGHLIGHTS You might just find yourself trailing behind a cattle drive on this trip through a bucolic remnant of California from, it seems, the early 1900s. The serene beauty of oak woodlands, rocky hills of golden grass and the canyon and valley of Deer Creek combine to make this little mountain road one of the prettiest in the foothills of the southern Sierra. You can combine this with Old Hot Springs Road (Tour 11).

DIFFICULTY Easy, on a narrow, maintained 2WD dirt road.

TIME & DISTANCE 1 hour; 18.2 miles.

MAPS ACSC's *Tulare County* (H–J, 6–8). *CRRA* p. 86 (H, 1–2).

INFORMATION Tulare County.

GETTING THERE **From the south (as described below):** At Fountain Springs (north of Bakersfield) take paved Hot Springs Road east toward California Hot Springs. In 7 miles you can detour onto Old Hot Springs Road (a.k.a. West Old Control Drive or M-52, Tour 11) by turning left (north) **[N35°52.966' W118°48.664']**. Just follow it for 10.8 miles to where it rejoins Hot Springs Road **[N35°52.278' W118°42.392']**. Then go left (northeast) and drive about 0.4 mile. Where Hot Springs Road bends east, bear north onto Tyler Creek Road **[N35°52.536' W118°42.053']**. Just across Tyler Creek, angle left (west) onto Deer Creek Drive **[N35°52.956' W118°42.017']**. Zero your odometer.

    From the north: Make your way to Magnolia (north of Bakersfield and south of Porterville), and then to Avenue 120. Follow it west, and it will become M-120, or MTN-120, which bends north to become Road 296. Just north of the bend, turn east onto Deer Creek Drive, also called Deer Creek Road, or M-112 **[N35°59.564' W118°54.655']**.

REST STOPS Sequoia National Forest's Leavis Flat campground, just across the forest boundary off Hot Springs Road.

THE DRIVE From the south, this narrow, one-lane mountain road, a genuine bit of bygone California where you almost expect to encounter a bouncing stagecoach or chugging Model T, twists along a canyon wall's sheer drop-off high above Deer Creek. If you look south across the canyon, you will see Old Hot Springs Road, or West Control Drive, edging along the canyon as well.

    Deer Creek Drive eventually crosses a ridge, then drops into a valley and crosses Deer Creek. The pastoral valley's hills and fields are strewn with countless granite boulders and outcrops, and oaks are everywhere. About 16 miles from Hot Springs Road, Deer Creek Drive widens, and the steep Sierra foothills you traveled through earlier diminish to lower, gentler hills. At about mile 18.2 is paved road MTN-120 **[N35°59.526' W118°54.643']** south of Porterville.

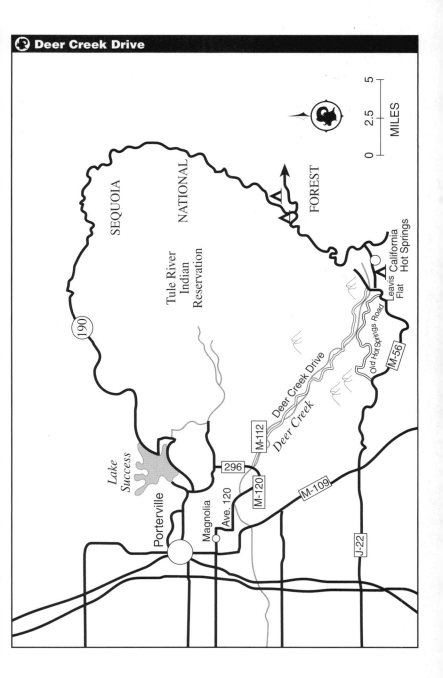

Old Hot Springs Road

LOCATION Tulare County, southeast of Porterville.

HIGHLIGHTS This is a thrilling, highly scenic and serpentine old shelf road high on the wall of a canyon in the foothills of the southern Sierra. You can make a terrific loop by combining this with nearby Deer Creek Drive (Tour 10).

DIFFICULTY Easy, on a 2WD dirt road.

TIME & DISTANCE 40 minutes; 10.8 miles.

MAPS ACSC's *Tulare County* (H–J, 7–8). *CRRA* p. 93 (A, 9–10).

INFORMATION Tulare County.

GETTING THERE **From Fountain Springs, north of Bakersfield (as described below):** Take Hot Springs Road east for 7 miles, then turn left (north) onto Old Hot Springs Road, a.k.a. Old Control Drive and MTN-52 **[N35°52.966' W118°48.664']**. Zero your odometer there.

    From Porterville: Take beautiful Deer Creek Drive (Tour 10) to Hot Springs Road. Take Hot Springs Road west for about 0.4 mile, then turn right (north) onto Old Hot Springs Road, or Old Control Drive **[N35°52.278' W118°42.392']**, and take the tour in the opposite direction.

REST STOPS Sequoia National Forest's Leavis Flat campground is just across the forest boundary off Hot Springs Road.

THE DRIVE Early on, a sign advises travelers that they are embarking on a narrow, winding road, and that is indeed true. It starts out crossing a flat expanse covered with scrub oak and grasses. After a mile or so it begins a gentle climb. To the west is a great view of the Central Valley, and ahead rise rugged Sierra foothills. By mile 3.7 the road has become a mere single-lane ledge supported in places by some interesting masonry work. The road twists along the southern wall of the canyon of Deer Creek. If you want to peer over the edge, stop and get out, lest you become part of the scenery down there yourself. By mile 10.7 you're on safer ground, and a short distance farther you're back on paved Hot Springs Road.

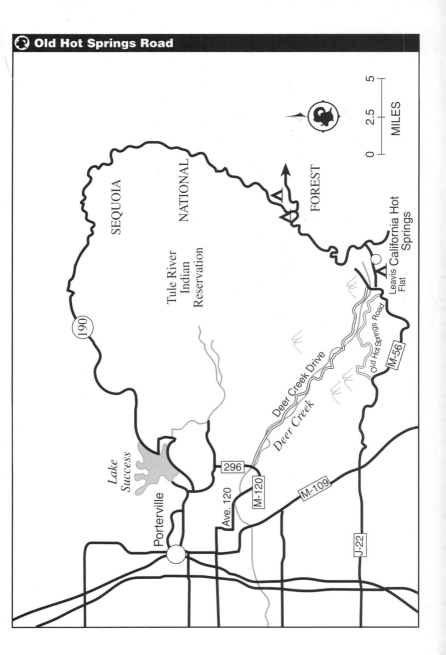

Rancheria Road

LOCATION Northeast of Bakersfield and west of Lake Isabella, in the Greenhorn Mountains of the southern Sierra. It extends between State Route 178 at the south end and State Route 155 at the north end. The northern section is in Sequoia National Forest. Kern County.

HIGHLIGHTS This scenic backroad climbs (or descends, if you go south) through pastoral remnants of old California, amid rolling foothills, oak woodlands and pine forests, with views into the canyon of Kern River. Oak Flat Lookout, built in 1934, provides vistas of the Kern River, Greenhorn Mountains and San Joaquin Valley. Evans Flat, named for 19th-century entrepreneur Robert Henry Evans, was a seasonal home for Native Americans for thousands of years. You can still see their grinding holes, called bedrock mortars, in the exposed rock where they ground acorns.

DIFFICULTY Easy, on a maintained 2WD road.

TIME & DISTANCE 3 hours; 37.5 miles.

MAPS *CRRA* p. 93 (B–E, 9–11). *Sequoia National Forest* (E–G, 11–13). ACSC's *Central Coast Region and Kern County* (A–B, 10–12).

INFORMATION Sequoia National Forest, Greenhorn Ranger District. Greenhorn Summit Ranger Station at the north end.

GETTING THERE **From the south (as described):** Take S.R. 178 (Kern Canyon Road) east from Bakersfield. About 3 miles east of the junction of State Routes 178 and 184, turn left (north) at a large orchard onto Rancheria Road (465) **[N35°24.969' W118°49.912']**, paved at this end for 4.2 miles. Zero your odometer.

   From the north: Take S.R. 155 (Forest Service Road 210) to Greenhorn Summit (west of Lake Isabella). Turn south onto Rancheria Road.

REST STOPS The Oak Flat Lookout can be rented for overnight stays (contact the Greenhorn Ranger District). Evans Flat campground is pleasant but has no drinking water. There's camping at Kern County Park, at the north end at Greenhorn Summit.

THE DRIVE After taking you 4.2 winding miles north from S.R. 178 into treeless hills, the pavement ends. The road takes you through oak woodlands dotted with old ranch buildings and granite outcrops. You started at about 820 feet above sea level, but after 11 miles you will have climbed above 3,000 feet. The views of the Central Valley at this point are outstanding.

   The road narrows to a single lane, and once again climbs steeply. Almost 15 miles from S.R. 178 is the short spur to Oak Flat Lookout **[N35°32.007' W118°42.455']**. (The road is closed at a gate in 0.4 mile; you have to walk the rest of the way.) Beyond that is a view of the Kern River. Rancheria Road comes to an intersection **[N35°36.351' W118°38.296']**; continue north toward Evans Flat and S.R. 155. Beyond that is the boundary of Sequoia National Forest, and a junction. Continue north to a Y junction, and stay on Road 465 (25S15) toward Greenhorn Summit.

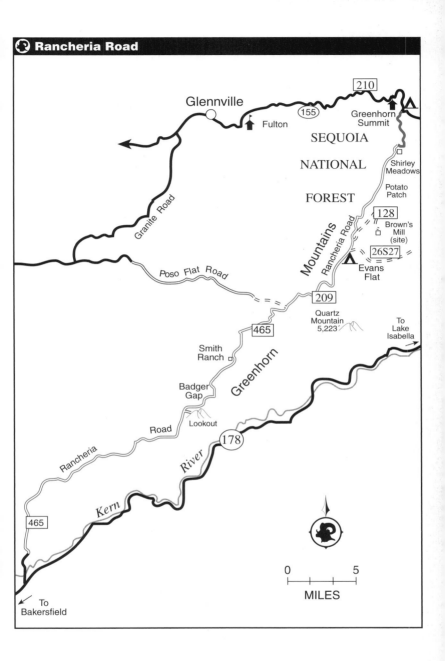

About 28.5 miles from S.R. 178 is Evans Flat campground, where you can view Native American bedrock mortars. For thousands of years, the Tabatulabal people came here to gather plants and hunt. A short distance farther is the junction with Sawmill Road. In about 5 miles you reach pavement at Shirley Meadows. S.R. 155 is 2.4 miles farther **[N35°44.267' W118°33.402']**, beyond an overlook above Isabella Lake.

Jawbone to Lake Isabella

LOCATION Piute Mountains of the southern Sierra Nevada; east of Bakersfield and north of Tehachapi. Between State Route 14 south of Red Rock Canyon State Park and Bodfish, near Lake Isabella. Sequoia National Forest. Kern County.

HIGHLIGHTS You will experience the transition from the Mojave Desert to the forests of the southern Sierra as you climb from 2,500 feet to over 8,000 feet. The descent to Kern Valley and Bodfish via a narrow shelf road is spectacular.

DIFFICULTY Easy.

TIME & DISTANCE 3 hours; almost 54 miles.

MAPS ACSC's *Central Coast Region* (A–B, 12–14). *CRRA* p. 94 (A–F, 1–4). At Jawbone Station, get a copy of *East Kern County Off-Highway Vehicle Riding Areas & Trails*.

INFORMATION BLM's Jawbone Station information center, near the junction of Jawbone Canyon Road and S.R. 14. Sequoia National Forest, Greenhorn Ranger District.

GETTING THERE From the east: From S.R. 14 about 1.1 miles south of Red Rock-Randsburg Road, take the Jawbone Canyon/Kelso Valley exit to Jawbone Canyon Road **[N35°18.001' W118°00.043']** and follow it west.

From the west: Take paved Caliente-Bodfish Road (483) to a point 2.8 miles **[N35°34.102' W118°30.404']** south of Bodfish, turn east onto Saddle Spring Road and make an exhilarating ascent.

REST STOPS BLM's Jawbone Station. You will find all services at Bodfish and Lake Isabella.

THE DRIVE Jawbone Canyon Road passes through an off-highway vehicle area. Pavement ends about 4.1 miles from S.R. 14, after you pass two large pipelines of the Los Angeles Aqueduct. Ahead is a green-blue hill, Blue Point **[N35°19.238' W118°04.962']**, which you'll reach at mile 4.7. Shortly beyond it, the road bends north and climbs into semiarid foothills, providing outstanding vistas across the Mojave Desert. The hills become dotted first with Joshua trees, then pinyon pines and junipers, then oak woodlands and conifers—changes that signal the transition from one climatic zone to another. The road descends into pretty Kelso Valley, passing a minor junction at mile 17.7. Following the sign that states PIUTE MOUNTAIN, continue on the main road to the major intersection just up ahead, at mile 18.1 **[N35°22.662' W118°13.024']**.

Kelso Valley Road goes north here. But follow Jawbone Canyon Road (589) west through the intersection. The road bends southwest and crosses a meadow. Then it turns west and climbs into the Piute Mountains. From there you ascend the steep and narrow switchbacks of Geringer Grade and enter Sequoia National Forest. Continue north to the junction with Piute Mountain Road (501) and Forest Service Road 27S02 (Saddle Spring Road/Piute Mountain Road) at mile 31.5 **[N35°26.640' W118°19.569']**. Turn left (west). At mile 33.4 **[N35°27.582' W118°20.745']**, bear left onto 27S02. At mile 37.2 **[N35°26.881' W118°22.698']**, bear right (north) on Saddle Spring Road. It eventually makes a thrilling descent to paved Caliente-Bodfish Road (483) **[N35°34.102' W118°30.404']**, just south of Bodfish at mile 53.7.

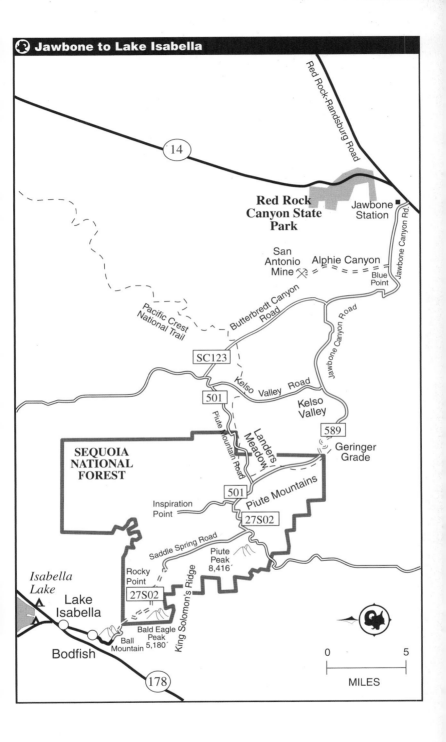

Chimney Peak Byway

LOCATION The tour circles Chimney Peak in the southern Sierra, near Sequoia National Forest between Kennedy Meadow Road and State Route 178, northeast of Lake Isabella. Tulare and Kern counties.

HIGHLIGHTS This drive through the southern Sierra Nevada wildlands is a Bureau of Land Management National Back Country Byway. It loops around 7,990-foot Chimney Peak, passing through more than 50,000 acres of federally designated wilderness in a transition zone between the Sierra Nevada and the Mojave Desert.

DIFFICULTY Easy. The BLM classifies this a Class II byway of narrow, slow-speed secondary roads suitable for high-clearance vehicles. Segments of the southern portion of Long Valley Loop Road are paved. Unpaved segments can be washboarded. Some sections may be impassable in winter and early spring.

TIME & DISTANCE 2.5–3 hours and 44 miles, beginning and ending at S.R. 178. About 1.5 hours and 25 miles for Long Valley Loop Road, beginning and ending at Nine Mile Canyon Road.

MAPS *CRRA* p. 94 (A–B, 3–4). *Sequoia National Forest* (K–L, 9–11). Bring the BLM's flyer *Chimney Peak Back Country Byway: A Passage Through Changing Times,* which identifies and explains points of interest. You may find some at the kiosk on Canebrake Road just off S.R. 178.

INFORMATION BLM's Bakersfield Field Office.

GETTING THERE **From the south (as described here):** Take S.R. 178 to Canebrake Road (20 miles east of Lake Isabella, and 18 miles west of State Route 14). Turn north onto Canebrake Road **[N35°44.925' W118°06.746']**.

　　From U.S. 395: Take the Kennedy Meadow turnoff (32 miles south of Olancha), and follow Nine Mile Canyon Road west for 11.7 miles. Turn left (west) onto unpaved Long Valley Loop Road **[N35°52.153' W118°00.788']** where the paved road bends north and becomes Kennedy Meadow Road.

REST STOPS Long Valley campground, off Long Valley Loop Road, and Chimney Creek campground, along Canebrake Road. Neither has drinking water.

THE DRIVE Serpentine Canebrake Road climbs along mountainsides above South Fork Valley and Chimney Creek. To the west is the Domeland Wilderness; to the east is the Owens Peak Wilderness. There are turnouts where you can take in the vistas, but don't expect guardrails.

　　After about 9 miles you come to the junction with the almost 20-mile-long Long Valley Loop Road **[N35°48.887' W118°03.234']**, an even narrower and twistier mountainside road that makes a spectacular loop high above Long Valley between the Domeland and Chimney Peak wildernesses, coming out at Kennedy Meadow Road. You can take it now, or continue winding north to Kennedy Meadow Road and take the loop road in the opposite direction **[N35°52.904' W118°02.910']**. Either way, the two ends of the unpaved byway are about 0.5 mile apart on Kennedy Meadow Road. The scenery and solitude along this lonely backroad is superlative no matter which way you go.

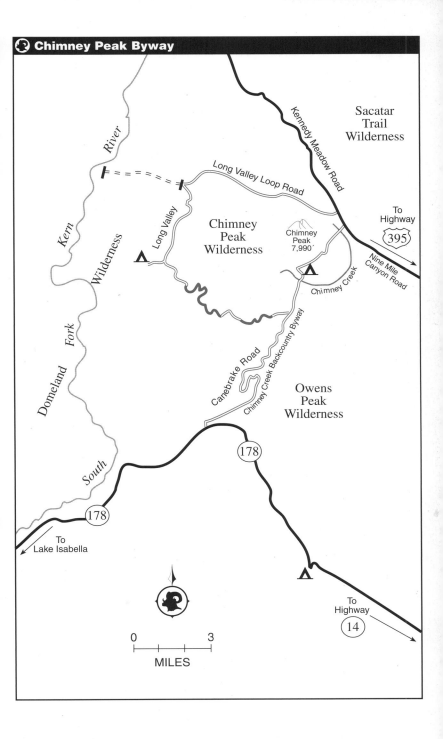

Sacatar
Trail
Wilderness

Kennedy Meadow Road

Long Valley Loop Road

River

Kern

Wilderness

Long Valley

Chimney
Peak
Wilderness

Chimney
Peak
7,990'

To
Highway
395

Nine Mile
Canyon Road

Chimney Creek

Fork

Donneland

Canebrake Road

Chimney Creek Backcountry Byway

Owens
Peak
Wilderness

178

South

178

To
Lake Isabella

To
Highway
14

0   3

MILES

Cherry Hill Road

LOCATION Sequoia National Forest, north of Lake Isabella, west of the Domeland Wilderness and south of Sherman Pass Road. Tulare County.

HIGHLIGHTS This pleasant cruise takes you through high, picturesque mountain meadows flanked by granite peaks and forest. The side trip to the Brush Creek Overlook provides outstanding vistas across the southern Sierra.

DIFFICULTY Easy.

TIME & DISTANCE 2 hours and 37 miles round-trip to Big Meadow. There are areas to explore south of Big Meadow that can add another hour or two.

MAPS *CRRA* pp. 86 (H, 5) and 94 (A, 1–2). *Sequoia National Forest* (H–J, 9). ACSC's *Tulare County* (G–J, 10–11).

INFORMATION Sequoia National Forest, Cannell Meadow Ranger District.

GETTING THERE Take Sherman Pass Road east for 4.7 miles from the junction with Sierra Way (Kern River Road). Turn south onto Cherry Hill Road (22S12) **[N35°58.977' W118°25.377']** and zero your odometer.

REST STOPS Horse Meadow campground.

THE DRIVE Much of the pleasure of this drive lies in getting to it, because Sherman Pass Road is just spectacular. Cherry Hill Road, which is paved for the first 5.7 miles, follows Poison Meadow Creek south through a forested area watered by numerous small streams. Almost 2 miles from where the pavement largely ends, the road to scenic Brush Creek Overlook (23S14) branches left (northeast) **[N35°55.452' W118°23.213']**. This narrow dirt road ends in almost 3 miles, at a turnaround area **[N35°57.086' W118°23.488']**. Park there, and walk through the trees to a rocky knoll from which you can gaze out at the rugged mountain expanse. From this turnoff, Cherry Hill Road continues south past its 8,833-foot-high namesake, which stands east of the road, and Horse Meadow, where you'll find a developed campground **[N35°54.104' W118°22.289']**.

Now the road descends into a landscape dotted with granite. Eventually you will see Big Meadow, and the prominent summit of 9,470-foot Cannell Peak. Continue to South Big Meadow Road **[N35°52.417' W118°21.075']**, which makes a scenic 5.9-mile loop that returns to Cherry Hill Road, passing two trailheads leading into the Domeland Wilderness. This is as far as I take you, but you can continue south to Long Meadow, Little Cannell Meadow, Rattlesnake Meadow and the logged region called Bartolas Country.

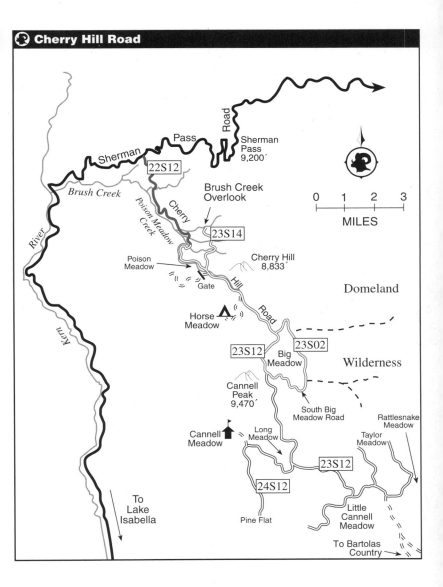

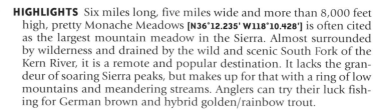

Monache Meadows

LOCATION Southwest of Olancha (on U.S. 395), along the South Fork of the Kern River, in Inyo National Forest (although you have to pass through Sequoia National Forest to get there). It's bordered on the west and north by the Golden Trout Wilderness, and on the east by the South Sierra Wilderness. Tulare County.

HIGHLIGHTS Six miles long, five miles wide and more than 8,000 feet high, pretty Monache Meadows **[N36°12.235' W118°10.428']** is often cited as the largest mountain meadow in the Sierra. Almost surrounded by wilderness and drained by the wild and scenic South Fork of the Kern River, it is a remote and popular destination. It lacks the grandeur of soaring Sierra peaks, but makes up for that with a ring of low mountains and meandering streams. Anglers can try their luck fishing for German brown and hybrid golden/rainbow trout.

DIFFICULTY Easy to moderate. The road is narrow and in places requires maneuvering between trees. The South Fork of the Kern River, just a stream here, may be deep in early summer. The route usually opens to motor vehicles by July.

TIME & DISTANCE 4–5 hours; about 25 miles round-trip from where the pavement ends.

MAPS *CRRA* p. 86 (E–F, 5–6). *Sequoia National Forest* (J–K, 7–8). USGS's *Monache Mountain* topo map.

INFORMATION Inyo National Forest, Mt. Whitney Ranger Station.

GETTING THERE **From the east:** Take the Kennedy Meadows turnoff from U.S. 395 (32 miles south of Olancha), onto Nine Mile Canyon Road. Follow the signs for Sequoia National Forest's Black Rock Work Station (37 miles), to the junction with Sherman Pass and Black Rock roads. (Nine Mile Canyon Road will become Kennedy Meadow Road.) **[N36°05.564' W118°15.833']**.

From the west: Take Sherman Pass Road northeast to the junction with Kennedy Meadow Road, near the Black Rock Work Station.

From the junction of Kennedy Meadow and Sherman Pass roads: Drive north on Blackrock Road (21S03) about 3.5 miles. Turn right (east) onto paved Road 21S36, at the sign for 4WD Monache Meadows Road (a.k.a. Sherman 4WD Trail) **[N36°07.693' W118°15.614']**. Note your odometer. At the Y junction in 3.5 miles **[N36°09.367' W118°14.489']**, bear left (north) and go through the gate. The pavement ends here. Zero your odometer.

REST STOPS There are primitive campsites in Monache Meadows.

THE DRIVE The road through a forest of fir and pine is well-maintained for the first mile. Beyond a pack train staging area, the route turns into a rocky, undulating 4WD trail that climbs and descends. At about mile 1.4 you may encounter a rough section. At mile 2.6 is a ledgy section to crawl down as you enter Bull Meadow **[N36°10.467' W118°12.661']**. Just beyond Bull Meadow, go through a gate, ford Snake Creek **[N36°10.757' W118°12.524']** and enter Inyo National Forest. Round a bend to the east, and Monache Meadows soon appears ahead. From here the road over Summers Ridge to the meadows area and the river is obvious.

Alabama Hills

LOCATION At the base of the Sierra Nevada, west of Lone Pine. Inyo County.

HIGHLIGHTS The Alabama Hills are a jumbled expanse of huge, rounded, honey-brown granite boulders with one of the region's most spectacular backdrops: the peaks of the Muir Crest, which culminate at 14,495-foot (according to the Inyo National Forest map; 14,494 according to the U.S. Geological Survey) Mt. Whitney, the highest point in the contiguous United States. The Alabama Hills have been a favorite stage for moviemakers and advertisers since the 1920s and a favorite venue for photography and rock climbing. Wildflowers add to this convenient drive during the first two weeks or so of May.

DIFFICULTY Easy, on graded roads. Spurs are rougher.

TIME & DISTANCE An hour; 13 miles.

MAPS *Inyo National Forest*. ACSC's *Eastern Sierra Guide Map*, Southern Region (AA, 3–4). *CRRA* pp. 86–87 (B, 6–7).

INFORMATION BLM's Bishop Field Office. Eastern Sierra InterAgency Visitors Center, just south of Lone Pine at U.S. 395 and State Route 136.

GETTING THERE From U.S. 395 at Lone Pine, take Whitney Portal Road west, directly toward the mountains, for 2.7 miles. Turn right (north) onto Movie Road **[N36°35.737' W118°06.533']**.

REST STOPS Fuel, food and lodging are available in Lone Pine. There are a number of campgrounds in the area. Dispersed camping in the Alabama Hills is discouraged.

THE DRIVE Just follow the easy, scenic semiloop through the 30,000-acre, Bureau of Land Management–managed Alabama Hills Recreation Area, a landscape of dramatic contrasts. Soaring to the west are the peaks of the eastern Sierra, sculpted by glaciers and the effects of water freezing and thawing in the granite's cracks and crevices. The Alabama Hills, however, consist of massive jointed and faulted boulders. They are almost identical in age and composition to the Sierra but are thought to have been shaped by chemical weathering when the climate was wetter and the rocks were buried.

In 1862, a precursor of the fictional Western shootouts filmed here occurred when settlers attacked a Paiute Indian camp, killing 11. When Confederacy sympathizers found gold here, they named their claims the Alabama District, after the Confederate Navy cruiser *Alabama*, which sank 64 Union merchant ships during the Civil War. Union sympathizers countered by naming their mining district, a town, a mountain and a pass after the Union's *Kearsarge*, which sank the *Alabama* in June 1864 off the port of Cherbourg, France. Since the 1920s, Hollywood has made the Alabama Hills familiar to moviegoers as the setting for numerous Westerns and other films—it even made a brief appearance in the 2000 film *Gladiator*. The area initially crossed by the road has been involved in so many films that it's dubbed Movie Flat.

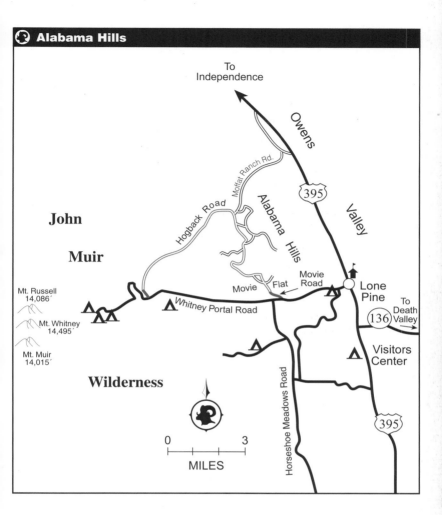

Hollywood has used the Alabama Hills' High Sierra backdrop in Westerns for decades.

Gunga Din is one of many films produced among the granite boulders of Alabama Hills, at the foot of the High Sierra.

Armstrong Canyon

LOCATION At the eastern edge of the John Muir Wilderness in Inyo National Forest, about 13 miles northwest of Independence. Inyo County.

HIGHLIGHTS Following Division Creek Road from the floor of the Owens Valley, this route zigzags up the dramatic eastern wall of the Sierra Nevada. It follows a narrow shelf road, an old mining road that leads past the sites of two bygone mines and ends at the remains of an old mine trolley, complete with a rusting ore car, in piney Armstrong Canyon. In addition to sweeping views of the Owens Valley, the Inyo Mountains and the Great Basin, you travel through a landscape where glacial canyons and boulder fields as well as ancient lava flows recall the region's fire-and-ice past.

DIFFICULTY Moderate, on a narrow single-lane shelf road carved into the steep side of the mountains. It is a bit off-camber in places, which can be disconcerting. Here and there, especially at one point as it enters Armstrong Canyon, the road is pinched between boulders on one side and long drop-offs on the other. Watch for oncoming vehicles and places to pass. Uphill traffic has the right of way, although that might not be practical in every case. Be prepared to back up if you encounter another vehicle, or a boulder that's fallen from the mountain and blocked the road.

TIME & DISTANCE About 5 hours and 18 miles round-trip from the start of Division Creek Road **[N36°56.065' W118°15.408']**.

MAPS *CRRA* p. 79 (J, 9–10). *Inyo National Forest*, South Half (J, 11).

INFORMATION Inyo National Forest, Mt. Whitney Ranger District.

GETTING THERE From the south: Take U.S. 395 a little more than 8 miles north from Independence. Exit onto Black Rock Springs Road (a.k.a. Sawmill Creek Road). Zero your odometer. Drive west 0.8 mile, then turn right (north) on Tinnemaha Road, following the U.S. Forest Service sign for the Sawmill Pass Trailhead. At about mile 1.9, turn left (northwest) onto Division Creek Road, toward a power plant, and zero your odometer again.

From the north: Take U.S. 395 south from Big Pine for about 16.4 miles, then exit at Goodale Creek Road (a.k.a. Goodale Road). Zero your odometer. Take Goodale Creek Road west a mile to Tinnemaha Road. Turn left (southwest) on Tinnemaha Road, follow it southwest 2.9 miles, and turn right onto Division Creek Road. Zero your odometer.

REST STOPS At mile 4.2 **[N36°56.235' W118°19.413']**, where the road bends sharply to the right (north), a left spur goes a short distance to a primitive campsite amid a grove of large oaks and cottonwoods at Scotty Spring. Primitive camping also is available at the end of this route, in a beautiful area below tall pines at about 8,300 feet, in Armstrong Canyon. Inyo County's pleasant Taboose Creek Campground, where a small fee is charged, is about 1.5 miles north of Goodale Creek Road, and the Bureau of Land Management's more open Goodale Creek campground, which also charges a fee, is in that vicinity as well.

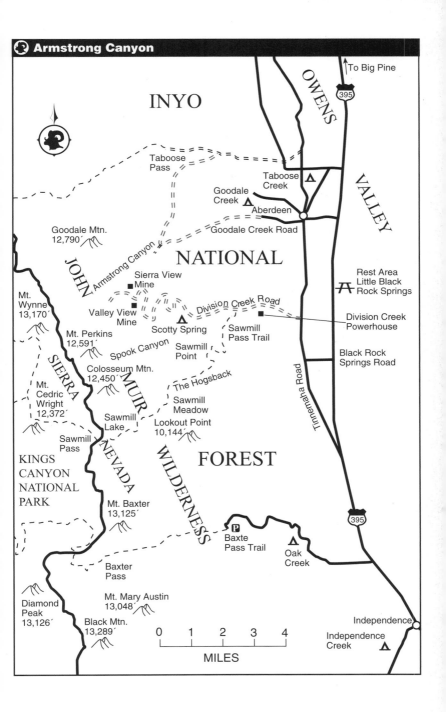

INYO

OWENS

To Big Pine

395

Taboose
Pass

Taboose
Creek

VALLEY

Goodale
Creek

Aberdeen

Goodale Mtn.
12,790′

Goodale Creek Road

NATIONAL

JOHN

Armstrong Canyon

Sierra View
Mine

Rest Area
Little Black
Rock Springs

Mt.
Wynne
13,170′

Valley View
Mine

Division Creek Road

Division Creek
Powerhouse

Mt. Perkins
12,591′

Scotty Spring

Sawmill
Pass Trail

Black Rock
Springs Road

SIERRA

Spook Canyon

Sawmill
Point

Colosseum Mtn.
12,450′

Mt.
Cedric
Wright
12,372′

The Hogsback

MUIR

Tinnemaha Road

Sawmill
Lake

Sawmill
Meadow

Sawmill
Pass

Lookout Point
10,144′

FOREST

KINGS
CANYON
NATIONAL
PARK

NEVADA

WILDERNESS

Mt. Baxter
13,125′

Baxte
Pass Trail

395

Oak
Creek

Baxter
Pass

Diamond
Peak
13,126′

Mt. Mary Austin
13,048′

Black Mtn.
13,289′

Independence

Independence
Creek

0   1   2   3   4

MILES

The old mining road to Armstrong Canyon edges along the escarpment of the eastern Sierra.

THE DRIVE The pavement ends at mile 1.5, where you will see the small Division Creek hydroelectric powerhouse on the left. From here the dirt road continues its steady climb toward the Sierra's steep granite escarpment and peaks that exceed 13,000 feet. At mile 2 the Sawmill Pass Trailhead is on the left (south) side of the road. This hiking trail (a wilderness permit is required for overnight stays but not for dayhikes) ascends via Sawmill Lake (about 7.4 miles) to the trail's namesake on the boundary of the John Muir Wilderness and Kings Canyon National Park (1.5 miles or so beyond the lake), then continues into the park. North of the road is the vast lava flow, which you'll edge along farther up.

Road 12S01 in Inyo National Forest bends sharply to the right (north) at mile 4.2. Here, the left branch continues to the primitive campsite at Scotty Spring noted under "Rest Stops." At this junction, you're right at the base of the Sierra escarpment. Your route continues through brush, and ascends along the mountainside. While the roadbed is good, at mile 4.5 it may be a bit off-camber, meaning the vehicle will tilt toward the downhill side. Less than a mile farther the drive brings you to the edge of the great lava flow. A good pullout to take in the view is just up ahead, at a switchback.

From here you continue to climb. At mile 7 **[N36°56.508' W118°20.302']**, on the left, are the diggings of the Valley View Mine. The shelf driving ends (temporarily) a half mile farther, and the road bends southwest into the mountains. From here you will have terrific views into Armstrong Canyon, your destination.

Mile 8.1 **[N36°56.705' W118°20.552']** brings you to the site of Sierra View Mine and a three-way junction. The right branch goes to a knoll with a fabulous view from just over 8,000 feet. The little-used left goes to some diggings. Take the middle road, clearly the most heavily used branch. It continues directly into Armstrong Canyon.

By mile 8.5 you are back on a shelf road again. You may encounter a particularly tight spot where boulders take up a portion of the road. (My 4Runner and a friend's Land Cruiser-based Lexus LX450 squeezed through.) The road ends at mile 9 **[N36°56.789' W118°21.219']**, at a primitive campsite sheltered by tall pines. You'll see an old ore car and other relics of the mine workings here.

Inyo Mountains

LOCATION East of the Sierra Nevada. Inyo County.

HIGHLIGHTS With the geologically linked White Mountains (Tour 21), the Inyos form the eastern wall of 10,000-foot-deep Owens Valley. Not as high as the Sierra or the Whites, they still provide an exhilarating driving experience. In addition to views of the Inyos' canyons and ridges, you have magnificent vistas across the Owens Valley to the Sierra. You will exit at Death Valley Road (a.k.a. Saline Valley/Eureka Valley Road. The route runs along the western and northern boundary of the Inyo Mountains Wilderness and connects to Tour 20 (The Narrows and Papoose Flat) at Papoose Flat, where the granite outcrops are reminiscent of the Alabama Hills in the Owens Valley, and where you can visit a natural arch.

DIFFICULTY Easy to moderate, with a steep and loose uphill segment, two short sidehill segments, and a rough downhill section leading to Papoose Flat. There are many spurs, some of which may get you off-course.

TIME & DISTANCE 7–8 hours; about 64 miles from Independence to Big Pine, including the side routes mentioned.

MAPS *Inyo National Forest,* South Half (K–L, 9–12). *CRRA* p. 79 (E–H, 11–12). ACSC's *Eastern Sierra Guide Map,* Southern Region (W–Y, 4–6) covers the route to Mazourka Peak.

INFORMATION Inyo National Forest's Mt. Whitney Ranger Station. The Eastern Sierra InterAgency Visitors Center at U.S. 395 and State Route 136, south of Lone Pine.

GETTING THERE Just south of Independence, turn east from U.S. 395 onto Mazourka Canyon Road (13S05) **[N36°47.828' W118°11.775']**. Zero your odometer.

REST STOPS There are good primitive campsites at Badger Flat and elsewhere. No water or facilities are available.

THE DRIVE When you reach the mountains, veer left (north), following dirt Mazourka Canyon Road up the canyon, an unusual cleft in that it runs north-south instead of the usual east-west. At mile 12.3 is the left (west) turn for road 13S05A **[N36°54.005' W118°05.127']** to Santa Rita Flat, which has great views from a number of easy roads.

   About 18.1 miles from U.S. 395 you come to Badger Flat **[N36°58.004' W118°05.554']**; bear left. In another mile is a right turn **[N36°58.761' W118°06.274']** that you will follow later, so make a note of it. Bear left, and in 0.3 mile bear left again **[N36°58.840' W118°06.636']**, onto a small road (11S01) that ascends about 1.3 miles to an awesome view from 9,412-foot Mazourka Peak. From there, return to that right fork you noted earlier. **Note or zero your odometer reading here.** Angle northeast past a corral, and in 0.5 mile—or 0.1 mile beyond the ruins of Blue Bell Mine **[N36°58.939' W118°06.004']**—turn left **[N36°58.885' W118°05.938']**. There may be a sign for Papoose Flat. Climb a steep, loose section toward a saddle. After going down a dip, crossing two side hills, you will meander high on a ridge with terrific views, then descend to a small valley and junction at mile 2.7

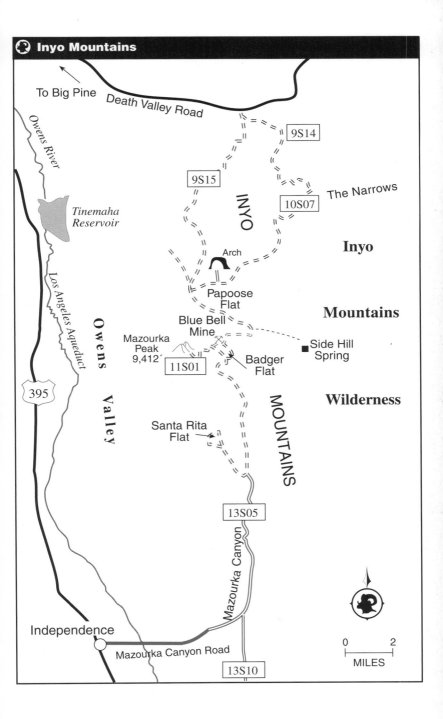

To Big Pine

Death Valley Road

9S14

9S15

Owens River

INYO

The Narrows

10S07

Tinemaha Reservoir

Inyo

Arch

Mountains

Papoose Flat

Los Angeles Aqueduct

Blue Bell Mine

Side Hill Spring

Mazourka Peak 9,412´

11S01

Badger Flat

395

Owens Valley

Wilderness

Santa Rita Flat

MOUNTAINS

13S05

Mazourka Canyon

Independence

Mazourka Canyon Road

0   2
MILES

13S10

Badger Flat, in the Inyo Mountains, provides views west across Owens Valley to the High Sierra.

[N36°59.344' W118°04.659']. The track to the northwest (left) from the valley floor is your route (9S15). **Note or zero your odometer again.**

In another 2.3 miles the road may seem to vanish, but it's to the left. Descend what may be a rough section to Papoose Flat, at about mile 3.4 **[N37°00.925' W118°07.276']**. Follow 9S15 north across Papoose Flat. Bear right in a short distance, at the Y junction just beyond the junction with Road 10S07, and continue to the switchbacks that lead down to paved Death Valley/Saline Valley/Eureka Valley Road **[N37°07.370' W118°04.659']**. From there, Big Pine is 13 miles to the left (west), via this road and State Route 168.

To visit the natural arch in Papoose Flat, as soon as you emerge onto the flat turn right (east), onto Road 10S07, and drive almost a half mile to the obvious little dirt road that branches off to the left (north). The arch **[N37°01.124' W118°06.779']** is at this short spur's end.

The Narrows
and Papoose Flat

LOCATION Inyo Mountains, southeast of Big Pine. Inyo County.

HIGHLIGHTS This beautiful loop includes an especially appealing mix
of very narrow, high-walled canyons leading to a particularly tight
gap called The Narrows (you won't drive through them). It continues to broad Papoose Flat, a lofty (about 8,400 feet) expanse that
has been a food-gathering place for American Indians for thousands
of years. It is marked by numerous massive granite outcrops (including one with an arch) that are reminiscent of the Owens Valley's famous Alabama Hills, with views across the 10,000-foot-deep valley
to the Sierra. At Papoose Flat you will connect with Tour 19 (Inyo
Mountains).

DIFFICULTY Easy. The canyon bottom is rocky and sandy in places.
This is a well-marked route.

TIME & DISTANCE 3.5 hours; 25.5 miles.

MAPS *Inyo National Forest,* South Half (K–L, 9–11). *CRRA* p. 79 (E–F, 11).

INFORMATION Mt. Whitney Ranger Station, Inyo National Forest.

GETTING THERE Take State Route 168 east from U.S. 395 at Big Pine.
In 2.2 miles turn right (southeast) onto paved Death Valley Road
(a.k.a. Saline Valley Road and Big Pine to Death Valley Road). In
another 11.2 miles turn right (south) at the sign for Papoose Flat
[N37°07.370' W118°04.659']. Set your odometer to 0.

REST STOPS The arch at Papoose Flat is a pleasant place to take a
break. There are many primitive campsites.

THE DRIVE In 0.1 mile you will come to a Y junction **[N37°07.250'
W118°04.581']**, the start of the loop. From here you can go in either
direction. The left branch (9S14, the way described below) follows
a long, narrow and serpentine canyon to The Narrows **[N37°04.485'
W118°01.600']**, then continues to Papoose Flat and returns to this
point. The southbound branch (9S15) of the Y junction makes the
loop in the opposite direction.

At the Y junction, take the left (eastward) branch (9S14) into
the hills. At mile 1.9 you are in a wash, and by mile 2.2 the roadway
narrows to a high-walled ravine. Watch for large rocks in the roadway here. By mile 3.5 the roadway narrows yet again, bends left, and then
climbs to a divide. Then it descends into another narrow canyon. At
about mile 6.2 you see some old mine buildings. The spur to the left
is the entrance to The Narrows, a high-walled gap in the dark, lami-
nated rock (schist) that leads into adjacent Marble Canyon. From
The Narrows, the road becomes 10S07, and runs along the western
boundary of the Inyo Mountains Wilderness.

At mile 8.7 you will come to a four-way junction **[N37°03.514'
W118°03.314']**, where Road 10S07 merges with Road 9S14. Turn left
(south) (right or north, if you're going in the opposite direction).
When you reach mile 9.7, Road 9S14 branches left **[N37°02.593'
W118°03.237']**. Bear right here, and begin a winding, sometimes sandy
5-mile drive through a region strewn with granite boulders. At the

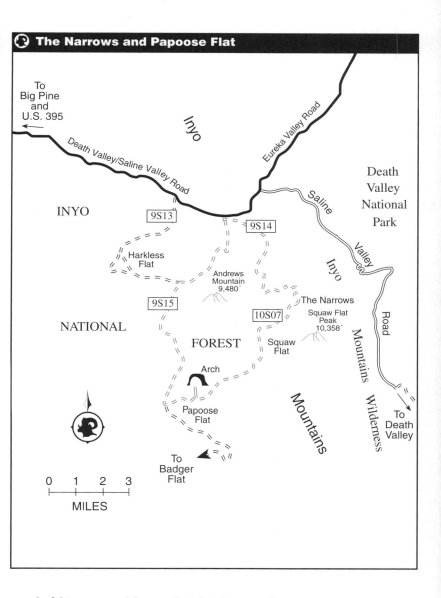

To
Big Pine
and
U.S. 395

Inyo

Eureka Valley Road

Death Valley/Saline Valley Road

Death
Valley
National
Park

INYO

9S13

9S14

Saline

Harkless
Flat

Andrews
Mountain
9,480´

Inyo

Valley

9S15

The Narrows

10S07

Squaw Flat
Peak
10,358´

NATIONAL

FOREST

Squaw
Flat

Arch

Mountains

Road

Papoose
Flat

Mountains

Wilderness

To
Death
Valley

To
Badger
Flat

0   1   2   3

MILES

end of this segment (about mile 14) is Papoose Flat **[N37°01.086' W118°06.102']**. By mile 14.3 you should see a short two-track road on the right (north), leading to a massive granite outcrop **[N37°01.124' W118°06.779']** where you can see a large arch in the granite.

A half mile beyond this turn is the junction with Road 9S15 **[N37°00.925' W118°07.276']**. If you turn left (south), a moderate 4WD trail climbs to Badger Flat, part of the Inyo Mountains tour. For the current tour, note your odometer reading (it should be at 15.1) and turn right (north). In about 5.4 miles (mile 20.5) is the left turn **[N37°04.831' W118°06.826']** to Harkless Flat, via a steep trail. From here, your route descends via switchbacks to the Y junction where you began the loop, and Death Valley/Saline Valley Road. From there, Big Pine is 13 miles to the left (west), via this road and S.R. 168.

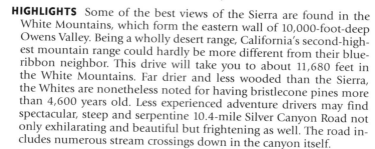

Silver Canyon
and the White Mountains

LOCATION East of Bishop. Mono and Inyo counties.

HIGHLIGHTS Some of the best views of the Sierra are found in the White Mountains, which form the eastern wall of 10,000-foot-deep Owens Valley. Being a wholly desert range, California's second-highest mountain range could hardly be more different from their blue-ribbon neighbor. This drive will take you to about 11,680 feet in the White Mountains. Far drier and less wooded than the Sierra, the Whites are nonetheless noted for having bristlecone pines more than 4,600 years old. Less experienced adventure drivers may find spectacular, steep and serpentine 10.4-mile Silver Canyon Road not only exhilarating and beautiful but frightening as well. The road includes numerous stream crossings down in the canyon itself.

DIFFICULTY The primary roads atop the Whites are easy gravel, but there is one hazard—flat tires. Be sure your spare tire is in good shape. I rate the upper 3.9 miles of Silver Canyon Road (6S02) moderate going uphill, but only because it's steep and narrow with tight switchbacks. It involves no technical four-wheeling. The lower 6.5 miles are easy, but there are numerous fordings, some of them surprisingly deep. I recommend going downhill so you can enjoy views of the canyon, Owens Valley and the Sierra. White Mountain Road from State Route 168 to Schulman Grove is paved.

TIME & DISTANCE All day; about 68 miles from U.S. 395 at Big Pine to U.S. 395 at Bishop. Silver Canyon Road is 11.4 miles from U.S. 6 to the top, with about 6,400 feet of elevation gain or loss, depending on your direction of travel. Accessible from June to October, the hike to White Mountain Peak is a strenuous, 15-mile (round-trip) trek from a locked gate at White Mountain Road's northern terminus **[N37°33.483' W118°14.203']**. The gate, a worthwhile destination due to its lofty, rugged and treeless setting, blocks vehicle access to the University of California's Barcroft Laboratory, where studies of the effects of altitude on animal physiology are conducted.

MAPS *Inyo National Forest* (J–K, 6–9). *CRRA* p. 79 (A–E, 9–11). ACSC's *Eastern Sierra Guide Map*, Southern Region (O–S, 7–9).

INFORMATION Inyo National Forest, White Mountain Ranger Station. The visitors center at Schulman Grove.

GETTING THERE **From U.S. 395 at Big Pine (descending Silver Canyon Road):** Drive northeast on S.R. 168 toward Westgard Pass. About 12.7 miles from Big Pine, turn north on White Mountain Road **[N37°39.111' W118°31.267']**.

From Bishop (ascending up Silver Canyon Road): About 3.8 miles northeast of town on U.S. 6, turn east on Silver Canyon Road (6S02) **[N37°23.995' W118°21.145']**. The gates on the roads leading into the White Mountains are closed in winter.

REST STOPS You will find no water, fuel or services. Grandview Campground (8,500 feet) is 5.4 miles north of S.R. 168 on White Mountain Road. Schulman Grove has the oldest known bristlecones, a

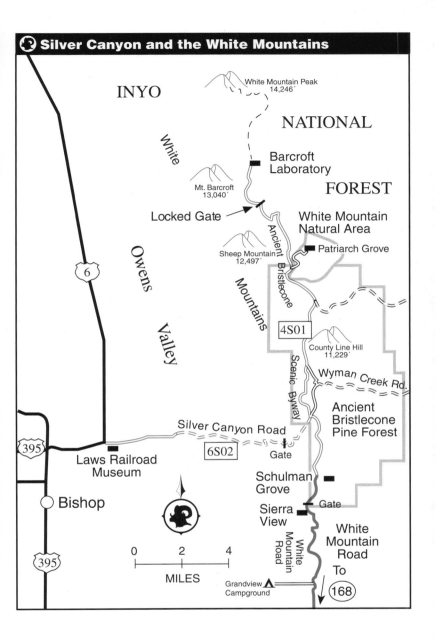

INYO

White Mountain Peak
14,246´

NATIONAL

White

Barcroft
Laboratory

FOREST

Mt. Barcroft
13,040´

Locked Gate

White Mountain
Natural Area

Ancient

Sheep Mountain
12,497´

Patriarch Grove

Bristlecone

Owens

Mountains

4S01

County Line Hill
11,229´

Valley

6

Scenic Byway

Wyman Creek Rd.

Ancient
Bristlecone
Pine Forest

Silver Canyon Road

395

6S02

Gate

Laws Railroad
Museum

Schulman
Grove

Gate

Bishop

Sierra
View

White
Mountain
Road

White Mountain Road

0   2   4

MILES

To

Grandview
Campground

168

395

The sparsely vegetated White Mountains, almost as high as the neighboring Sierra, are home to ancient bristlecone pines.

visitors center, trails and a picnic area. Patriarch Grove has the largest known bristlecone and picnic tables. Some who plan to hike to White Mountain Peak camp at the locked gate; check with the Forest Service for restrictions.

THE DRIVE The White Mountains present an uncommon mix of driving experiences, from the scenic thrill of Silver Canyon to the other-worldly, sparsely vegetated crest. At many points the views of the Sierra rank among the most inspiring sights in the West.

The Whites contrast starkly with the Sierra. While the two ranges formed simultaneously, they are geologically, climatically and visually distinct. The well-watered and forested Sierra is generally glaciated granite, an igneous rock. The Whites appear almost barren but for pinyon-juniper woodlands and, higher up, the hardy, gnarled bristlecones. They are composed primarily of sedimentary rock 500 million to 600 million years old. While fossils are scarce in the Sierra, fossils nearly 600 million years old are found in the White Mountains. Standing in the rain shadow of the Sierra, these mountains lack the precipitation that formed glaciers in the Sierra.

On the crest, skyscraping White Mountain Road, a.k.a. Ancient Bristlecone Scenic Byway, winds through rocky mountaintops to end at a locked gate at the north end, at about 11,680 feet. Hikers can climb from there to White Mountain Peak, at 14,246 feet California's third highest. From the top of Silver Canyon **[N37°24.990' W118°11.429']**, at about 10,480 feet, you can access beautiful, easy-to-moderate Wyman Creek Road **[N37°26.408' W118°11.186']**, which ends in Deep Springs Valley in about 16 miles with numerous stream crossings.

Coyote Flat
and Coyote Ridge

LOCATION Inyo National Forest southwest of Bishop. Inyo County.

HIGHLIGHTS The drive goes from semiarid Owens Valley, at about 4,400 feet, to Coyote Flat, a vale more than 10,000 feet high that lies below the Palisade Group's 13,000- to 14,000-foot peaks. The steep slopes, sharp crest, glacial remnants and perennial snowfields of the Sierra's second highest cluster of peaks make them an inspiring sight. (The Muir Group, which includes 14,495-foot Mt. Whitney, is the highest.) Tucked among the peaks are Palisade Glacier, the Sierra's largest, and Middle Palisade Glacier. Palisade Glacier is visible from a high spur road on the east side of the valley that is described below, and Middle Palisade Glacier is prominently visible from Coyote Flat. From Coyote Flat, you can continue up to and over 11,400-foot-plus Coyote Ridge to an overlook with superlative views of the glaciated High Sierra. The return drive provides vistas across the 10,000-foot-deep Owens Valley to the White Mountains, highest in the Great Basin. From Coyote Flat, you can hike to Baker Lake, in the John Muir Wilderness, from the Baker Creek Trailhead. There are a number of 4WD spurs to explore as well.

DIFFICULTY Easy to moderate, with narrow sections and switchbacks. Spurs can be rocky and steep, and I rate them generally moderate.

TIME & DISTANCE All day, or better yet spend a weekend; 55 miles or more round-trip, depending on how much exploring you do.

MAPS *CRRA* p. 79 (C–E, 8–9). *Inyo National Forest* (G–H, 8–9). AC-SC's *Eastern Sierra Guide Map,* Southern Region (Q–S, 4–5). Also useful are the USGS's 7.5-minute *Coyote Flat* and *Mt. Thompson* topo maps.

INFORMATION Inyo National Forest, White Mountain Ranger Station.

GETTING THERE From Main Street (U.S. 395) in downtown Bishop, follow West Line Street (State Route 168) west for 1.5 miles. Turn left (south) onto South Barlow Lane, drive 1 mile, then turn right (west) onto Underwood Lane. After just over 0.8 mile, where the road curves to the right (northwest), turn left (south) **[N37°20.795' W118°26.327']** onto Coyote Flat Road, a.k.a. Coyote Valley Road, 7S10 on the Forest Service map. Set your odometer at 0.

REST STOPS There are many undeveloped but established campsites. The best is a large area amid a stand of pines at the southwestern edge of Sanger Meadow, at the southern end of Coyote Flat just beyond Cow Creek. Bring a portable toilet. You also can camp or picnic at Coyote Lake and the trailhead for the hike to Baker Lake. Both have pit toilets.

THE DRIVE Bear right just before the power substation, drive under the power lines and head directly toward the lofty, craggy peaks. The road is quite sandy as it winds through low, rocky sagebrush-covered hills. Then it passes through a ravine and climbs toward a canyon. Mile 3.3 brings you to the boundary of Inyo National Forest.

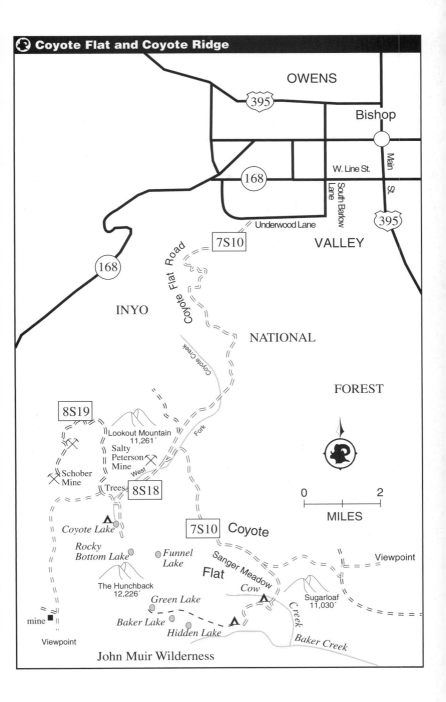

OWENS

Bishop

395

168

W. Line St.

Main St.

South Barlow Lane

395

Underwood Lane

VALLEY

7S10

Coyote Flat Road

168

INYO

Coyote Creek

NATIONAL

FOREST

8S19

Lookout Mountain
11,261'

Salty
Peterson
Mine

West Fork

Schober
Mine

Trees

8S18

0   2

MILES

Coyote Lake

7S10   Coyote

Rocky
Bottom Lake

Funnel
Lake

Sanger Meadow

Viewpoint

Flat

The Hunchback
12,226'

Cow

Sugarloaf
11,030'

Green Lake

Creek

mine

Baker Lake

Hidden Lake

Baker Creek

Viewpoint

John Muir Wilderness

A 4WD side road ascends to a breathtaking viewpoint near Sugarloaf, in the foreground, high above Coyote Flat.

At mile 3.9 there is a spur to the right; keep left **[N37°18.857' W118°29.338']**. The road, a shelf carved into the mountainside, now becomes steep and rocky as it makes a long, serpentine ascent amid steep, boulder-strewn canyons. The views of Owens Valley and the White Mountains to the east evolve from great to amazing. A series of switchbacks begins at mile 4.2, then at mile 5, where the road bends into the mountains, a steep section has been crudely paved and the shelf driving ends. Now you're at about 7,000 feet, in a pinyon-juniper woodland. At about mile 7.6 a spur to the left goes a short distance to a knoll of granite boulders. Scramble up them on foot for a terrific view across Owens Valley.

By mile 9.6 you arrive on the crest of a ridge, where you are suddenly gazing at high, open rolling hills and soaring Sierra peaks. Cross aspen-lined Coyote Creek at mile 10.7 or so, and follow the road up the draw. Long and wide Coyote Flat finally comes into view by mile 12.

At about mile 12.4 (or 12.1 if you didn't take the knoll cited back at mile 7.6) the road brings you to the left turn **[N37°14.628' W118°29.605']** to Coyote Flat, Sanger Meadow, Cow Creek and Baker Creek via road 7S10. Note your odometer, turn left here, and cross the West Fork Coyote Creek. (Note that you will return to this junction with Road 8S18 to explore Coyote Ridge.)

Keep to the left at mile 14.7 or so, where a sign may indicate that Baker Creek is to the left. By about mile 15.5, on the right, is the signed road toward Funnel Lake. It becomes very rocky after crossing what used to be a dirt airstrip, and essentially ends well before reaching the lake. It's worth exploring only if you have time to spare.

About 1.8 miles beyond this junction a small road (moderate) branches to the left (east) **[N37°11.762' W118°27.288']**. (Another entrance to the same road is a few yards farther ahead.) It's a good single-lane road up the eastern wall of the valley. For an inspiring view that stretches from the John Muir Wilderness, including Palisade Glacier, to the west, and east across Owens Valley and into the Great Basin, this 1.9-mile (one-way) side trip can't be beat. It ascends to a ridge, then drops into a grassy basin and runs along the base of 11,030-foot Sugarloaf. About 1.4 miles from Road 7S10, it reaches a T intersection **[N37°11.576' W118°25.975']**. Turn left (northwest), and in 0.2 mile turn right. After you're sure you're in 4WD and low range, make the steep climb to the crest of the ridge and the viewpoint **[N37°11.943' W118°25.837']**.

Back on 7S10, continue southeast another 1.8 easy miles, toward the stunning, snowy peaks of the Palisade Group—including 14,012-foot Middle Palisade Peak and its glacier—that rise above a stand of tall pines at the southwestern corner of the valley. You cross the tiny wooden bridge over Cow Creek, enter Sanger Meadow, then find yourself in an undeveloped camping area amid tall pines **[N37°10.608' W118°26.960']**. The road makes a sharp rightward bend here. Note your odometer at this point.

To reach the trailhead for the worthwhile hike to beautiful Baker Lake **[N37°10.101' W118°28.861']**, continue on this road (moderate) for another 0.8 mile, to a Y junction. Bear left on the road that descends in the direction of the Palisade Group. Then bear right at mile 1. The wooded trailhead for Baker Lake is about 2.2 miles from the undeveloped camping area. It's a moderately difficult hike that takes about 40 minutes one-way.

To explore the Coyote Ridge area, backtrack the length of Coyote Flat (6.7 miles) and return to the junction back at about mile 12.4, where you turned off the road that brought you up from Owens Valley and crossed West Fork Coyote Creek. Zero or note your odometer, and turn left (southwest) on Road 8S18. You pass the site of the bygone Salty Peterson Mine **[N37°13.886' W118°30.109']** and continue along West Fork Coyote Creek (crossing it at 1.9 miles) for 2.4 miles to a signed junction **[N37°13.081' W118°31.176']**. As the sign states, the left branch, still 8S18, goes to Coyote Lake—a relatively humble

After crossing Coyote Ridge, the road ends at a viewpoint overlooking South Lake and the John Muir Wilderness.

body of water by Sierra standards, but still a pleasant place to stop—in 0.2 mile. Spurs from the lake lead to mine sites above it. The branch directly ahead from this junction continues to Coyote Ridge.

Zero your odometer at this junction and take the right branch, posted at the junction as road 8S19 but shown as 8S18 on the 2002 *Inyo National Forest* map. It bends to the right. At about mile 0.4 from the Coyote Lake junction bear left **[N37°13.216' W118°31.496']**. Road 8S19 branches off to the right (north) into some trees, leading eventually to the Schober Mine **[N37°14.441'W118°32.695']** in about 4.3 miles. Continuing to the left, you slowly ascend to about 11,400 feet on Coyote Ridge, which provides a sweeping vista. After descending from the ridge, at about mile 3.1 you see an old mine site at the end of a short spur to the right **[N37°11.954' W118°32.934']**; keep to the left. (This segment isn't depicted on the *Inyo National Forest* map.) Bear left again at about mile 3.4, following the rocky two-track. The road soon takes you across an open area, and by mile 3.7 or so it ends at a vista point **[N37°11.565'W118°32.985']** with a head-spinning view of the John Muir Wilderness and the jagged Sierra crest from about 10,600 feet, some 900 feet above South Lake and the canyon of the South Fork of Bishop Creek.

Buttermilk Country

LOCATION West of Bishop. Inyo County.

HIGHLIGHTS This drive takes you to the very foot of the eastern Sierra's soaring escarpment, one of the West's most dramatic sights. Particularly appealing, I think, is the contrast of the mountains' snowy, glaciated ramparts with the high sagebrush desert below, in this lofty divide's rain shadow. The views extend from peaks more than 13,000 feet high, east across 10,000-foot-deep Owens Valley to the White Mountains, highest in the Great Basin. The Buttermilks, a roadside cluster of massive granite boulders, are renowned in the sport of bouldering. The area is popular for mountain biking and hiking as well.

DIFFICULTY Easy to moderate. Spurs can be difficult.

TIME & DISTANCE Allow 1.5 hours for this 14.7-mile semiloop, without exploring spurs.

MAPS *Inyo National Forest*, North Half (G, 8). ACSC's *Eastern Sierra Guide Map*, Southern Region (Q, 3–5). *CRRA* p. 79 (C–D, 7–8).

INFORMATION Inyo National Forest, White Mountain Ranger Station.

GETTING THERE In central Bishop, drive west from U.S. 395 (Main Street) on West Line Street (State Route 168). In 7.3 miles, just inside the national forest, turn right, onto Buttermilk Road (7S01) **[N37°19.957' W118°31.297']**. Zero your odometer.

REST STOPS There are many places, including primitive campsites, along the way. There are campgrounds south of Buttermilk Country as well. Bishop has all services.

THE DRIVE I've heard two reasons for the name Buttermilk Country. One says teamsters from a sawmill on Birch Creek long ago would stop for a drink of buttermilk at a dairy. Another says that when 19th-century ranchers would haul goat milk to Bishop in the summer months, it would turn to buttermilk along the way. Today, visitors get to drink in pure scenic grandeur.

About 3.6 miles from S.R. 168, at a climbers' parking area **[N37°19.761' W118°34.779']** at the base of a group of massive boulders, Buttermilk Road diminishes to a single lane. Bear right at the fork just beyond the parking area. The road becomes rockier now as it angles southwest across a glacial moraine, and takes you gradually higher. If you've never felt dwarfed by nature before, this epic landscape should do it, for you are driving below the ramparts of such sentinels as Mt. Tom (13,652 feet), Basin Mountain (13,181 feet), Mt. Humphreys (13,986 feet) and Mt. Emerson (13,118 feet), which do their part to sap Pacific air currents of moisture, leaving little for the Great Basin to the east.

Bear right at mile 3.9. Soon the road heads south behind Grouse Mountain. At about mile 5.9, on the right, is road 701A **[N37°18.523' W118°36.515']**, the spur to the Horton Lake Trailhead. This high-clearance road takes you 1.3 miles to a locked gate near the boundary of the John Muir Wilderness, where there is some space for parking. A wilderness permit is required for overnight trips in the wilderness,

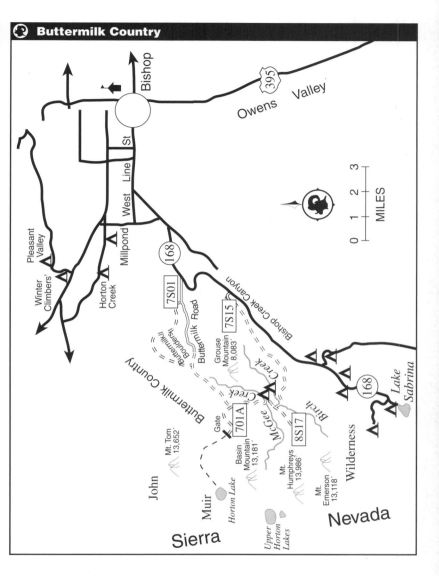

and mechanized travel is not allowed. This moderately strenuous trail ends in about 3.5 miles at Horton Lake **[N37°19.013' W118°39.831']**.

From the Horton Lake Trailhead turn, it's on through a stand of pines and aspens at mile 7.2, a change from the vast expanses of sage-covered high desert. The road crosses McGee Creek at mile 7.5 **[N37°17.172' W118°36.493']**, where there is an appealing primitive campsite amid the pines, then makes a steep but short climb out of the creek's ravine. Bear left at mile 8.1, where Road 8S17 branches right, toward the mountains. Beyond this spur, Buttermilk Road turns away from the mountains. Watch for another fine, woodsy primitive campsite at mile 9.1. Now the road makes a long, gradual descent on the crest of a narrow ridge that parallels S.R. 168 and Bishop Creek Canyon. It becomes quite rocky before reaching the highway at mile 14.7 **[N37°18.680' W118°31.362']** about 2.5 miles from where you began the drive.

Volcanic Tableland

LOCATION Owens Valley, north of Bishop between U.S. 395 and U.S. 6. Mono and Inyo counties.

HIGHLIGHTS The Volcanic Tableland, a gnarled expanse of boulders and serpentine ravines that is popular for the sport of bouldering, formed 700,000 years ago when vents of the Long Valley Caldera, to the northwest, spewed clouds of hot rhyolitic ash and rock. Visitors enjoy petroglyphs, the narrows of Red Rock Canyon and views of the Sierra and the White Mountains. The route passes through the Fish Slough Area of Critical Environmental Concern, a 36,000-acre area of wetlands, alkali meadows and uplands where the Mojave Desert and Great Basin converge. **Note:** Do not touch the petroglyphs.

DIFFICULTY Easy to moderate.

TIME & DISTANCE 3 hours; 52 miles.

MAPS *Inyo National Forest*, North Half (F–H, 5–7). *CRRA* p. 79 (A–C, 7–9). ACSC's *Eastern Sierra Guide Map*, Southern Region (O–Q, 5–7) and Northern Region (L–N, 5–7).

INFORMATION BLM's Bishop Field Office.

GETTING THERE In Bishop, take U.S. 6 north for 1.4 miles. Where it bends east, turn left onto Five Bridges Road. Drive 2.4 miles. After passing through a gravel yard and crossing a canal, turn right (north) onto Fish Slough Road (3V01) **[N37°25.173' W118°24.569']**. Zero your odometer.

REST STOPS Campers typically use the Bureau of Land Management's Horton Creek, a few miles west of Bishop (early May through November 1; $5 per site per night in 2008) or Pleasant Valley Pit, a.k.a. "The Pit," a short distance southwest of the west end of Chalk Bluff Road and west of Pleasant Valley Road (November 1 to early May; $2 per vehicle per night in 2008) campgrounds. Inyo County's nearby Pleasant Valley Campground, at the west end of Chalk Bluff Road, is more developed and pleasant, but charges a few dollars more ($10 per site per night in 2008).

THE DRIVE Fish Slough Road passes the only natural springs remaining on the floor of Owens Valley. At mile 6.7 **[N37°30.793' W118°24.868']** from where you turned onto Fish Slough Road is the first petroglyph site, where you can also see mortars, or grinding holes. The next site is 4 miles farther north **[N37°34.284' W118°25.061']**, behind a fence on the right after you drop into Chidago Canyon. The best site, Red Rock Canyon Petroglyphs, is another 5.6 miles north **[N37°39.027' W118°26.072']**, among the rocks to the left (west). A half mile north of there **[N37°39.400' W118°26.407']**, bear left (northwest) onto Chidago Canyon Road (3S53), toward Red Rock Canyon.

About a mile after Road 3S53 exits the canyon, it reaches a junction **[N37°39.111' W118°31.267']**. Road 3S53, or "Chidago Loop" as a sign might state, bends right (east). Note your odometer here. Go straight (southeast), taking 4S34 another 2.5 miles. Just before the point where 4S34 bends right (west), turn left (east) onto a small road, 4S41 **[N37°37.218' W118°32.199']**. (This is a good mountain-biking segment, although it's not a loop.) Zero your odometer again. Bear

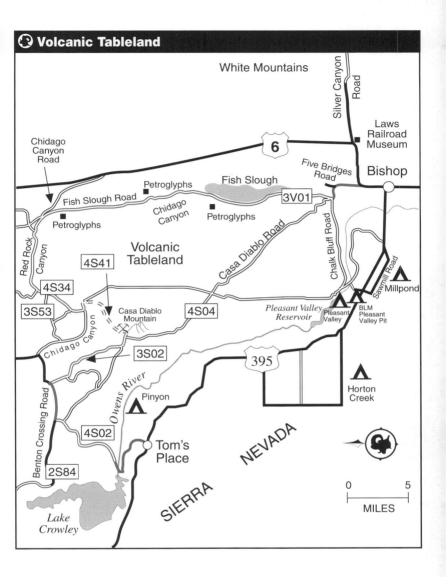

White Mountains

Silver Canyon Road

Laws Railroad Museum

Chidago Canyon Road

6

Five Bridges Road

Bishop

Petroglyphs

Fish Slough

Fish Slough Road

3V01

Chidago Canyon

Petroglyphs

Petroglyphs

Red Rock Canyon

Volcanic Tableland

Casa Diablo Road

Chalk Bluff Road

Sawmill Road

Millpond

4S41

4S34

3S53

Casa Diablo Mountain

4S04

Pleasant Valley Reservoir

Pleasant Valley

BLM Pleasant Valley Pit

Chidago Canyon

3S02

395

Owens River

Pinyon

Horton Creek

4S02

Tom's Place

NEVADA

Benton Crossing Road

2S84

SIERRA

0   5
MILES

Lake Crowley

right in 0.3 mile from Road 4S34. At about 1.1 miles from Road 4S34, after climbing into the piney volcanic hills, you are facing east toward the White Mountains. Turn right (south) here **[N37°37.032' W118°31.642']**, continuing on 4S41 and ignoring spurs.

At mile 2.8 is a rough downhill section with a great view of the Sierra. Once down it, bear left (south), and in 0.4 mile you reach the small track leading to Casa Diablo Mine, an early-20th-century gold mine. A short distance to the right is graded Casa Diablo Mine Road (shown on the Inyo forest map as both 3S02 and 4S04) **[N37°35.133' W118°33.965']**. You can take it southeast for 19 miles to Bishop. I suggest taking 3S02 north 6.7 miles to Benton Crossing Road (2S84) **[N37°38.672' W118°37.014']**. There, turn left (west). At Waterson Divide turn left (south) onto Owens Gorge Road (4S02) **[N37°38.243' W118°39.300']**, which meets U.S. 395 at Tom's Place.

Sand Canyon Road

LOCATION Inyo National Forest. The road runs along the eastern rim of Rock Creek Canyon northwest of Bishop and south of Tom's Place (on U.S. 395). It ends at the edge of the John Muir Wilderness. Mono County.

HIGHLIGHTS This drive provides outstanding views down into popular Rock Creek Canyon, and up at the John Muir Wilderness's chiseled, snowy peaks, which stand well over 13,000 feet. This is a popular downhill mountain-biking route as well. You can link it with more challenging Wheeler Ridge Road (Tour 26).

DIFFICULTY Moderate. There are some very rocky stretches. Brush extends into the roadway in some places as well.

TIME & DISTANCE 2.5 hours and 18.6 miles round-trip, excluding time spent at the lake.

MAPS *CRRA* p. 79 (B–C, 7–8). *Inyo National Forest* (F–G, 6–7). For greater detail bring the USGS's 7.5-minute *Mt. Morgan* and *Tom's Place.*

INFORMATION Inyo National Forest, White Mountain Ranger Station.

GETTING THERE Take U.S. 395 north of Bishop, then take the Lower Rock Creek Road (a.k.a. Old Sherwin Grade Road) to Swall Meadows Road **[N37°30.637' W118°37.296']**. Take Swall Meadows Road 0.6 mile, then turn right onto Sky Meadow Road. Follow Sky Meadow Road for 0.5 mile. At a gravel pit reset your odometer and take 4S54, the two-track road on the right **[N37°30.883' W118°38.291']**. In 0.7 mile it crosses Witcher Creek, then immediately bends left (west). Now you're on Sand Canyon Road (5S08).

REST STOPS There is a very pretty unnamed lake at the end of Sand Canyon Road. Stop at the cafe and store at Tom's Place.

THE DRIVE The road follows Witcher Creek to Witcher Meadow, then continues along Birch Creek into the narrow V formed by Sand Canyon. The roadbed is a coarse granitic sand, not the soft desert or beach sand that can require airing down substantially. The road climbs through pine trees, aspen and stretches of narrow brush. By mile 3.9 you're making a long, steep climb to the top of the canyon, at mile 4.4. There you can pause at a turnout to take in the stunning mountain vista at the head of Rock Creek Canyon. In another half mile, stop to look over the brink of the canyon, a busy place in summer with campgrounds, picnic areas and trailheads. At mile 5.4 is one of a number of rocky stretches where low range will be helpful. (Remember to keep your tires on the high points to avoid scraping your vehicle's undercarriage.) The roadside brush is quite close here as well, so your vehicle might acquire a pinstripe or two.

At mile 7 look up to your left at Wheeler Ridge, which can be crossed via Wheeler Ridge Road (a.k.a. Wheeler Crest Road & Wheeler Ridge Mine Road), a challenging 4WD road that branches to the left at mile 7.3 **[N37°28.391' W118°42.716']**. (It isn't on the *Inyo National Forest* map but is on the USGS's 7.5-minute *Mt. Morgan.*) At mile 8.8 is a rocky downhill pitch that requires care. You are rewarded at mile 9.3, when you arrive at a tranquil lake **[N37°27.655' W118°42.810']** with a terrific view of the soaring peaks of the John Muir Wilderness.

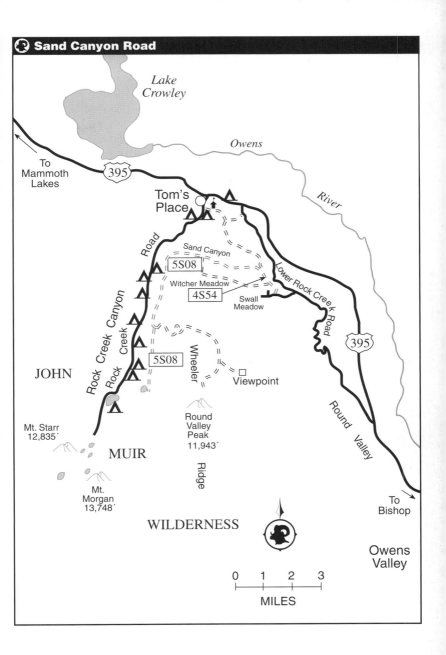

Lake
Crowley

Owens

395

To
Mammoth
Lakes

Tom's
Place

River

Road

Sand Canyon

5S08

Witcher Meadow

4S54

Swall
Meadow

Lower Rock Creek Road

395

Rock Creek Canyon

Rock Creek

5S08

Wheeler

Viewpoint

JOHN

Round Valley

Mt. Starr
12,835′

MUIR

Round
Valley
Peak
11,943′

Ridge

Mt.
Morgan
13,748′

WILDERNESS

To
Bishop

Owens
Valley

0   1   2   3

MILES

Wheeler Ridge Road

LOCATION Inyo National Forest between U.S. 395 and Rock Creek Canyon, northwest of Bishop and south of Tom's Place. Mono County.

HIGHLIGHTS Four-wheeling over an 11,000-foot ridge rewards you with views of glaciated peaks, Rock Creek Canyon and a high basin with a small lake and wind-blown sand dunes. At a vista point at the end **[N37°29.067' W118°40.374']** is a truly spectacular view across Owens Valley to the White Mountains.

DIFFICULTY This is the most challenging route in this book. Be prepared for some heavy lifting—you may well need to rearrange granite roadbed rocks at several difficult spots to make your way through.

The road up Sand Canyon Road (Tour 25), which you must take to reach the starting point of this drive, is moderate. The 2-mile stretch from Sand Canyon Road to the crest of Wheeler Ridge is difficult due to a number of substantial roadbed rock outcrops that you will have to work your way over and through slowly and carefully. Undercarriage scraping is likely at these sections. A locking rear differential, high clearance, experience and a good spotter will all be very helpful.

The road on the east side of the ridge, to the overlook where I end the drive, is moderate. I do not recommend driving beyond the overlook, which would involve a dangerous traverse on a very narrow mountainside shelf.

You will encounter ledges and very rocky spots that require good ground clearance, and are easier if your vehicle has a rear locking differential. Undercarriage scraping is possible. Portions of Sand Canyon Road are rocky, with roadside brush.

TIME & DISTANCE Consider this an all-day trip. From the start of Sand Canyon Road near Tom's Place to Wheeler Ridge Road is about 45 minutes and 7.4 miles one-way. From there, it's about 1.5 to 2 hours, and 3.4 miles, one-way to the overlook, including the spur to the dunes. If you combine this with the remainder of Sand Canyon Road, plan to spend 5 to 6 hours altogether on this trip at least, and add 4 miles. (Sand Canyon Road ends 2 miles beyond the junction with Wheeler Ridge Road.)

MAPS *CRRA* p. 79 (B, 7). *Inyo National Forest* (F–G, 6–7). USGS's 7.5-minute *Mt. Morgan* and *Tom's Place*. Sand Canyon Road is on the *Inyo National Forest* map, but Wheeler Ridge Road is not.

INFORMATION Inyo National Forest, White Mountain Ranger Station.

GETTING THERE Take Sand Canyon Road to Wheeler Ridge Road **[N37°28.391' W118°42.716']**.

REST STOPS Have lunch or camp at the undeveloped overlook.

THE DRIVE From Sand Canyon Road, follow Wheeler Ridge Road along a meadow and past granite outcrops. Cross a brook, then maneuver carefully between boulders and trees. A mile from the start the steadily ascending trail makes a bend to the right, at the first of a series of spots where you have to crawl, probably in low range, over difficult sections of roadbed rocks and small boulders. After

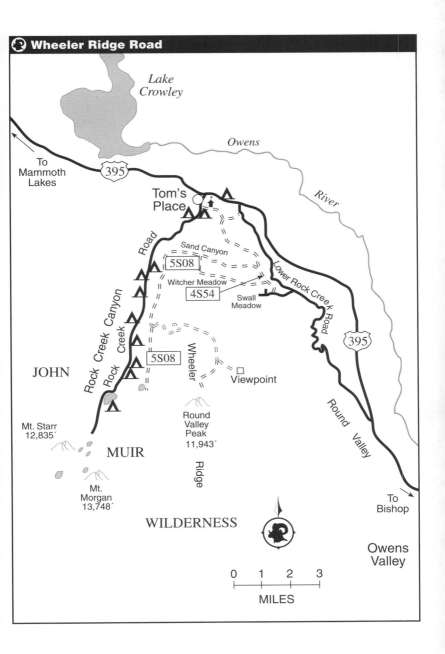

A storm approaches over Wheeler Crest, seen from the viewpoint above Owens Valley.

substantial uphill four-wheeling, mile 2 finds you at just about 10,950 feet on the crest of Wheeler Ridge **[N37°29.403' W118°41.393']**, looking down at an intriguing basin at more than 10,800 feet, with a small lake (which may be greatly diminished due to drought) **[N37°29.435' W118°41.186']** and rare sand dunes. The route is pretty easy from here.

Follow the road down to and across the basin, to a junction. The right branch, as you can see, goes a short distance to sand dunes pushed by wind against a mountainside—a rare sight in the High Sierra. The left, or main branch, descends eastward above a canyon, then bends south to reach another junction **[N37°29.096' W118°40.526']** about 0.6 mile from the basin. Below to the left is the viewpoint where I end the drive, at about 10,570 feet.

If you want to explore the mountainside 4WD trail ahead (it ends in about 3.1 miles at the John Muir Wilderness boundary), hike or bike it. From the turnoff to the viewpoint, it's about 0.6 mile to a small basin and another knoll. Here you can see how the salt-and-pepper, igneous granite is interspersed with chunks of black rock. The chunks are remnants of the primordial Earth's crust that broke off into the once-molten magma as it rose toward the surface and eventually became today's Sierra granite. It's worth the walk.

Laurel Canyon

LOCATION Inyo National Forest, south of Mammoth Lakes. Mono County.

HIGHLIGHTS This is a spectacular and convenient 4WD sojourn from U.S. 395 and Mammoth Lakes, up a glacial moraine and into a breathtaking glacier-carved canyon high on the Sierra's steep eastern escarpment. The views of the Long Valley Caldera (a 75-square-mile crater formed by a massive volcanic eruption 700,000 years ago), volcanic Mono Craters (formed 6,000 to 6,500 years ago) and other features of the Sierra's volcanic past are terrific. Aspens along Laurel Creek, which cascades down the bottom of the canyon, make it a good early-autumn drive. It ends at the head of the canyon, near two sparkling lakes (with trout fishing) at the edge of the John Muir Wilderness.

DIFFICULTY Moderate. The narrow, rocky road makes for a slow and bumpy ride. You will encounter switchbacks and one stretch along a talus slope. I've found the road blocked not far from the end by snow in late July, making for a tricky turnaround.

TIME & DISTANCE 3 hours; about 9 miles round-trip.

MAPS *CRRA* p. 78 (A, 5). *Inyo National Forest* (D, 5–6). *Mammoth Lakes Area Off-Highway Vehicle and Mountain Biking Map.* ACSC's *Eastern Sierra Guide Map,* Northern Region (K–L, 3).

INFORMATION Inyo National Forest, Mammoth Ranger Station and Visitors Center.

GETTING THERE A mile southeast of the Mammoth Lakes turnoff on U.S. 395, exit west onto Sherwin Creek Road. Drive west for 1.4 miles. Laurel Canyon Road (a.k.a. Laurel Lakes Road), 4S86, is on the left (southwest) side of the road **[N37°37.417' W118°54.394']**. You also can take Sherwin Creek Road from Old Mammoth Road at the town of Mammoth Lakes. At 4S86 set your odometer at 0.

REST STOPS There are primitive campsites in the canyon. You will find other camping areas, primitive and developed, in the vicinity of Mammoth Lakes, which has all services.

THE DRIVE You can see the long, high-walled glacial trough of Laurel Canyon, where the 4WD road winds up a large moraine, rising from about 7,400 feet to almost 10,000 feet. At mile 2.9 the narrow road crosses a steep talus slope on the canyon's southeastern wall. Ahead is a great view of Laurel Creek cascading down the canyon; behind you is Long Valley, a caldera; and to the north are the Mono Craters cones.

　　The road makes a couple of easy switchbacks. Soon you should be able to see whether the road is blocked farther up by snow, which tends to linger in the road on a north-facing slope at about mile 4.4 to 4.5. The road is relatively wide there. If it is blocked, you should be able to park and continue on foot, but be sure to leave room for other visitors. If the road is clear, continue a short distance to a wide and flat area that has room to park and turn around.

　　From this point the descent to the larger and prettier of the two Laurel Lakes **[N37°34.576' W118°54.785']** is very rough, with a tight switchback. The road here is likely to be obstructed by large rocks. Instead of trying to drive down to the larger lake, park and walk; it's about 20 minutes down and 30 minutes back up.

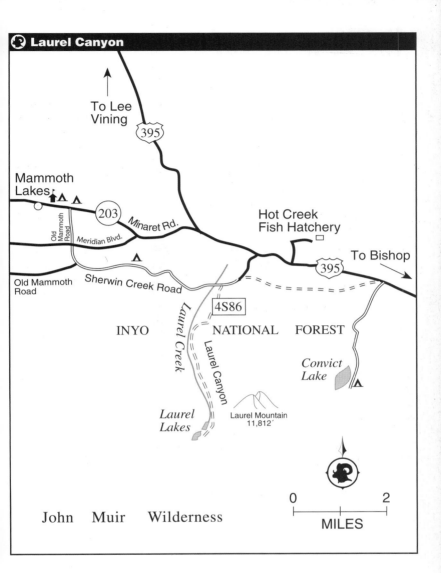

To Lee Vining

395

Mammoth Lakes

203 Minaret Rd.

Old Mammoth Road

Meridian Blvd.

Hot Creek Fish Hatchery

To Bishop

395

Old Mammoth Road

Sherwin Creek Road

4S86

INYO

Laurel Creek

Laurel Canyon

NATIONAL

FOREST

Convict Lake

Laurel Lakes

Laurel Mountain 11,812´

John   Muir   Wilderness

0   2

MILES

Long Valley Caldera

LOCATION Inyo National Forest east of Mammoth Lakes. Mono County.

HIGHLIGHTS You will cross the wooded, volcanic landscape of the 75-square-mile Long Valley Caldera and the desert in the Sierra's rain shadow. The summits of Lookout Mountain (8,352 feet) and Bald Mountain (9,104 feet) provide 360-degree vistas of a vast region, including the escarpment of the eastern Sierra, Mammoth Mountain (an 11,053-foot dormant volcano) and Mono Basin. There is quite a network of mountain-biking trails throughout the Mammoth Lakes area.

DIFFICULTY Easy, on high-clearance 2WD roads. Although there are many junctions, the important ones are marked.

TIME & DISTANCE It's about 4 hours and 53 miles from Mammoth Lakes to State Route 120 and 27 miles more to U.S. 395.

MAPS *CRRA* p. 73 (F–H, 10–12). *Inyo National Forest* (D–F, 3–5).

INFORMATION Inyo National Forest, Mammoth Ranger Station and Visitors Center, on the north side of State Route 203 at Mammoth Lakes.

GETTING THERE At Mammoth Lakes, turn north off S.R. 203 west of the Mammoth Ranger Station and Visitors Center, onto Road 3S08 **[N37°38.795' W118°57.833']**. Reset your odometer, and drive toward Shady Rest Park.

REST STOPS There are no services after Mammoth Lakes. Refer to your map for campgrounds.

THE DRIVE The pavement ends at Shady Rest Park. From there graveled Road 3S08 goes through piney forest to U.S. 395 **[N37°42.282' W118°57.073']**. There, you will see two small concrete tunnels that pass beneath the highway. (Check your clearance.) Once through the tunnels the road angles left (north) to Road 3S06 **[N37°42.581' W118°57.080']**. Turn right (east) onto 3S06, and in a short distance turn left (north) onto Road 2S02 **[N37°43.092' W118°56.804']**. It takes you 3 miles to the summit of Lookout Mountain **[N37°43.737' W118°56.852']**, where you can view the volcanic Mammoth region. Mammoth Mountain dominates a gap in the Sierra that lets moist Pacific air slip through, which creates Mammoth's famous heavy snowfall and waters the dense forest that spreads out into the desert from the gap.

Return to 3S06, and continue to 2S08 **[N37°43.555' W118°55.346']**. Follow 2S08 north to paved Owens River Road **[N37°44.875' W118°55.357']**, at Owens River Ranch. Turn left (west) there, then turn right (north) into Big Springs campground **[N37°44.860' W118°56.327']**. Keep to the right, and follow Road 2S04 up Alpers Canyon toward Bald Mountain Lookout **[N37°47.024' W118°54.064']**, about 10 miles away via Road 1S05.

As you climb Bald Mountain watch for a small road, 1S11, on the left **[N37°48.215' W118°54.061']**. Make a note of it, and continue to Bald Mountain Lookout. Then return to 1S11, note your odometer, and follow it east for 2.3 miles to Pilot Springs Road (1S04) **[N37°48.388' W118°52.356']**. You'll want to go east there. But for the moment, cross

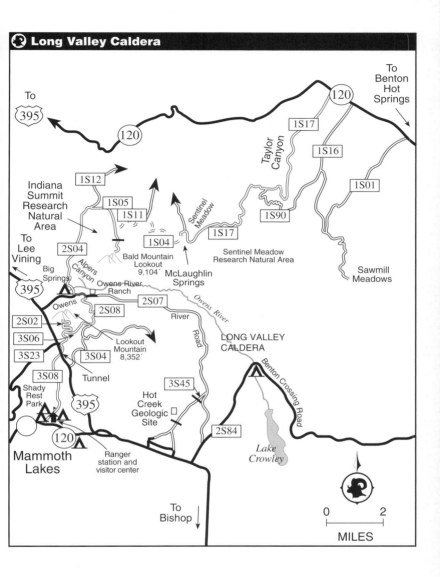

it and take the two-track ahead a short way to a rocky knoll with a great view. Then return to 1S04, note your odometer again, and continue southeast toward McLaughlin Springs **[N37°47.570' W118°50.189']**.

In 2.7 miles angle left at the bend, and climb to a ridge and a T intersection with Road 1S17 **[N37°47.954' W118°50.008']**. Note your odometer again, then turn right (south). Follow 1S17 over a ridge (note how chips of obsidian, a black volcanic glass, make the roadbed sparkle here). About 8.4 miles from that earlier T intersection, turn left (east) onto Taylor Canyon Road, a.k.a. Adobe Ranch Road (1S17) **[N37°50.027' W118°45.293']**. In 8.7 miles you will be at S.R. 120 **[N37°54.798' W118°41.344']**. U.S. 395 is about 27 miles to the left (west).

TOUR 29

San Joaquin Ridge

LOCATION West of Mammoth Lakes and north of State Route 203 (Minaret Road) at Minaret Summit. Inyo National Forest. Mono County.

HIGHLIGHTS This is a short yet terrific drive to over 10,000 feet, where you'll have a head-spinning 360-degree view. The volcanic soil is fragile, so stay on the road, which is popular for hiking and mountain biking as well as four-wheel driving.

DIFFICULTY Moderate. The road is steep and rutted in places, and winds between narrowly spaced trees near the start. I once found the road blocked by a large, shaded snowdrift late in July. Watch for hikers. Parking and turnaround space is tight at the road's end.

TIME & DISTANCE 1–1.5 hours; 5 miles round-trip.

MAPS *CRRA* p. 73 (H, 9). *Mammoth Lakes Area Off-Highway Vehicle and Mountain Biking Map,* available locally. The road is not shown on the *Inyo National Forest* map, but it's well-marked, well-established and easy to find and follow.

INFORMATION Inyo National Forest, Mammoth Ranger Station and Visitors Center, on the north side of S.R. 203 at Mammoth Lakes.

GETTING THERE From Mammoth Lakes, take S.R. 203 (Minaret Road) toward Minaret Vista and Devils Postpile, driving through the large parking area for Mammoth Mountain Resort. On Minaret Summit, just before the Minaret Vista entrance station, turn right (north) into a dirt area **[N37°39.230' W119°03.462']**. In a few yards the little San Joaquin 4WD road and bike trail angles left, toward Deadman Pass. Zero your odometer.

REST STOPS There are excellent vista points. Mammoth Lakes has all services. Minaret Vista has a picnic area with parking, tables, toilets and great views. Devils Postpile National Monument is nearby as well.

THE DRIVE Some steep climbing lies ahead, so shift into low range early. After 1.5 miles you reach a shaded spot that can be blocked by snow well into summer. If it is blocked, don't attempt to cross, and don't leave the road to get around it. If it's clear, the road exits the trees and climbs steeply to a ridge that provides a front-row view of the Minarets, 12 pointy peaks in the Ritter Range of the Sierra Nevada. Named for the towers on mosques, the Minarets are all that remain of a lava flow that predates today's Sierra. To the south looms 11,053-foot Mammoth Mountain, a dormant volcano formed some 370,000 years ago that now dominates a heavily forested gap in the Sierra's rain shadow. Here, moist air slips up the San Joaquin River drainage and through the gap to deliver the heaviest snowfall in the eastern Sierra, an average of 353 inches a year. Gaze east across the volcanic, 75-square-mile Long Valley Caldera, headwaters of the Owens River, to Glass Mountain Ridge, even to the distant White Mountains. About 2.5 miles from Minaret Summit the road ends at a blustery point overlooking Deadman Pass **[N37°41.309' W119°04.244']**.

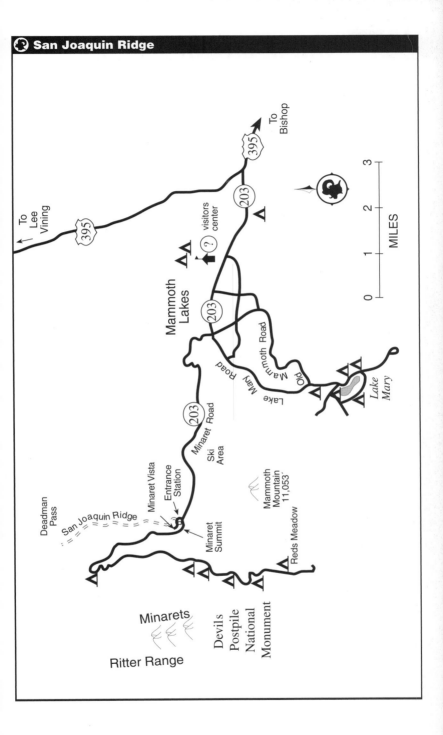

To Lee Vining

To Bishop

395

395

203

203

203

visitors center

Mammoth Lakes

Old Mammoth Road

Lake Mary Road

Lake Mary

Minaret Road

Ski Area

Mammoth Mountain 11,053'

Reds Meadow

Deadman Pass

San Joaquin Ridge

Minaret Vista

Entrance Station

Minaret Summit

Minarets

Devils Postpile National Monument

Ritter Range

MILES

0   1   2   3

Horse Meadows Loop

LOCATION   Southwest of Mono Lake and the junction of State Route 120 and U.S. 395, at Lee Vining. Inyo National Forest. Mono County.

HIGHLIGHTS   This short and convenient tour at the eastern edge of Yosemite National Park passes two pretty mountain meadows, Upper and Lower Horse Meadows, on a loop around 8,431-foot Williams Butte. Views reach from the volcanic Mono Craters to the peaks of the Ansel Adams Wilderness and Yosemite National Park. This loop is also a designated and well-marked mountain-biking trail, making it easy to follow—watch out for bikers.

DIFFICULTY   Easy.

TIME & DISTANCE   45 minutes; 6.5 miles.

MAPS   *CRRA* p. 73 (F, 8–9). ACSC's *Eastern Sierra Guide Map*, Northern Region (F, 3) or CSAA's *Sierra Nevada-Yosemite Area* (F, 9). Inyo National Forest's visitor map is useful, but it doesn't show the north-south connecting link that makes this a loop.

INFORMATION   Mono Basin Scenic Area Visitors Center, north of Lee Vining on U.S. 395.

GETTING THERE   About 1.2 miles south of the junction of S.R. 120 and U.S. 395, turn west onto Horse Meadows Road (1N16), at the sign for HORSE MEADOWS on the west side of U.S. 395 **[N37°56.273' W119°06.063']**. Set your odometer to zero.

REST STOPS   Any place you like. Nearby Lee Vining has all services. Refer to your maps for campgrounds in the area.

THE DRIVE   As soon as you pull off the highway and head west on Horse Meadows Road (1N16), you are looking up at snow-salted peaks as high as 13,053 feet (Mt. Dana). At mile 1.2, just beyond the junction with Aqueduct Road (1N17) **[N37°56.077' W119°07.085']**, you come to grassy Lower Horse Meadow. In another mile the road enters a narrow granite canyon, and then makes a short but steep climb on a chewed-up stretch. A short distance beyond that, at mile 2.8 or so, the road enters a stand of pines at the edge of a larger meadow, Upper Horse Meadow. (Continuing ahead for 0.7 mile will take you to the Gibbs and Kidney lakes Trailhead.)

Immediately upon entering the pines, turn left (south) **[N37°55.294' W119°08.475']**, and drive up to the crest of a ridge, where small roads branch left and right **[N37°55.186' W119°08.408']**. Continue straight ahead (south), and wind down the south side of the ridge, passing through a woodland strewn with large granite boulders. The views of the Sierra's dramatic eastern escarpment are spectacular as you descend and cross a couple of small streambeds. The route bends to the east, toward U.S. 395, and runs along the base of Williams Butte. Go through another junction with Aqueduct Road **[N37°54.388' W119°06.919']**, which comes in from the left (north) here, and soon you are on paved Oil Plant Road, which brings you to U.S. 395 **[N37°55.056' W119°05.829']**.

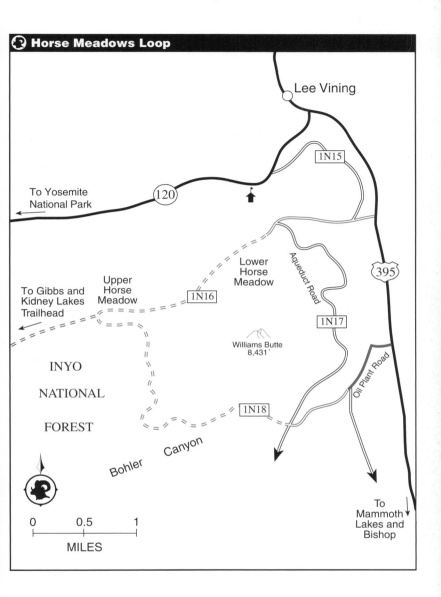

Lee Vining

1N15

120

To Yosemite
National Park

Lower
Horse
Meadow

Aqueduct Road

395

Upper
Horse
Meadow

To Gibbs and
Kidney Lakes
Trailhead

1N16

1N17

Williams Butte
8,431´

INYO

NATIONAL

1N18

FOREST

Oil Plant Road

Bohler   Canyon

To
Mammoth
Lakes and
Bishop

0   0.5   1

MILES

Hikers, mountain bikers and four-wheelers share the San Joaquin Jeep Road (Tour 29) near Mammoth Lakes.

Horse Meadows Loop (Tour 30) winds through pinyon-juniper woodlands.

Copper Mountain Loop

LOCATION Humboldt-Toiyabe National Forest. Northwest of Mono Lake. West of U.S. 395 and Conway Summit. Mono County.

HIGHLIGHTS This loop on Copper Mountain is a convenient side trip from U.S. 395 that provides outstanding vistas, from the eastern Sierra across volcanic Mono Basin and the Bodie Hills to the Great Basin. The route is great for mountain biking as well. It is particularly beautiful by about mid-September, when the aspens are turning their golden autumn color.

DIFFICULTY Easy.

TIME & DISTANCE 1 hour; 10.8 miles.

MAPS *CRRA* p. 73 (E, 8). *Toiyabe National Forest*, Bridgeport Ranger District (J, 15). CSAA's *Sierra Nevada-Yosemite Area* (E, 8–9). ACSC's *Eastern Sierra Guide Map*, Northern Region (D, 3).

INFORMATION Humboldt-Toiyabe National Forest, Bridgeport Ranger District. The Mono Basin Scenic Area Visitors Center, north of Lee Vining on U.S. 395.

GETTING THERE At Conway Summit, about 12 miles north of Lee Vining on U.S. 395, turn west on Virginia Lakes Road **[N38°05.250' W119°10.924']**. About 0.4 mile from the highway, turn left (southwest) onto Road 180, at a sign stating JORDAN BASIN **[N38°05.271' W119°11.379']**. Set your odometer at 0.

REST STOPS Lee Vining has all services. The Mono Basin Scenic Area Visitors Center has restrooms, books, maps and more. Mono Lake County Park, just off U.S. 395 at the northwest corner of Mono Lake, has picnic areas, bird-watching opportunities, a playground and restrooms. You will find camping, food, lodging and other amenities at Virginia Lakes and elsewhere in the area.

THE DRIVE The road quickly becomes rocky as it meanders up the slopes of Copper Mountain toward Mt. Olsen. Soon you get panoramic views of Mono Lake (one of the oldest bodies of water in North America), volcanic Mono Craters and other features formed over millions of years by glaciation, volcanic eruptions and faulting. You also have great views of the long spine of the High Sierra. In 2 miles Road 180 reaches Road 181 (on the left) **[N38°04.045' W119°12.491']**, which is where you will come out after completing the loop. Continue straight ahead.

At mile 3.2 is the other end of Road 181, on the left **[N38°03.405' W119°13.602']**. Take it. It climbs and winds in and out of forest, eventually bringing you to a crest with spectacular view of glacier-carved Lundy Canyon and the peaks of the Hoover Wilderness. At a junction at mile 5.5, go left **[N38°02.731' W119°11.943']**. In 0.4 mile **[N38°03.054' W119°11.787']** is another awesome vista point overlooking the Mono Basin. Return to the junction and follow Road 181 north. It passes through stands of large aspens, descending until it rejoins Road 180. Go right, and retrace your route to Virginia Lakes Road and U.S. 395.

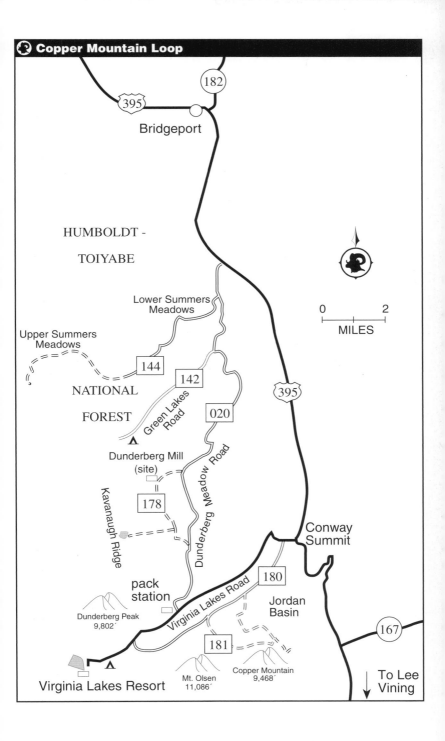

Dunderberg Meadow Road

LOCATION Humboldt-Toiyabe National Forest, northwest of Mono Lake and just west of the Hoover Wilderness. Mono County.

HIGHLIGHTS Aspen groves and high snowy peaks make this a very scenic drive and a great early autumn drive. There's a beautiful un-named lake (at about 10,250 feet) at the end of a short 4WD spur to the base of Kavanaugh Ridge. I highly recommend this tour as an alternate route if you're traveling on U.S. 395 and have some extra time. It can be combined with Copper Mountain Loop (Tour 31).

DIFFICULTY Easy and relaxing on a maintained road. The spur to the lake is moderate. The drive can be taken in either direction, but I think going north, the direction I describe, is the most scenic.

TIME & DISTANCE 1.5 hours; about 15 miles.

MAPS *CRRA* p. 73 (D–E, 8). *Toiyabe National Forest*, Bridgeport Ranger District (H–J, 14–15). ACSC's *Eastern Sierra Guide Map*, Northern Region (B–D, 3–4) or CSAA's *Sierra Nevada-Yosemite Area* (D–E, 8).

INFORMATION Humboldt-Toiyabe National Forest, Bridgeport Ranger District.

GETTING THERE From 8,138-foot Conway Summit, the highest point on U.S. 395, about 12 miles north of Lee Vining, turn west on Virginia Lakes Road. After about 4.5 miles turn right (north) onto Dunderberg Meadow Road (020) **[N38°03.382' W119°14.669']**, which merges with Green Lakes Road at the northern end near U.S. 395. Zero your odometer.

REST STOPS The unnamed lake at the base of Kavanaugh Ridge is a gorgeous place for a break. There are campgrounds at Virginia Lakes, and other amenities at Virginia Lakes Resort.

THE DRIVE Going north, Dunderberg Meadow Road begins as a graveled two-lane road. In less than a mile it narrows to a single lane, then winds through pines and across sage- and grass-covered foot-hills.

At mile 1.3 from Virginia Lakes Road turn left (west) off Dunderberg Meadow Road onto Forest Service Road 178 **[N38°04.640' W119°14.177']**. Follow Road 178 for 0.3 mile to a Y junction **[N38°04.925' W119°14.314']**. Take the left branch. (Road 178 is a rough little 4WD road that continues north through the forest to the site of the old Dunderberg Mill and then reconnects with the main road. There isn't much left of the mill except debris.) This spur is steep at first as it climbs through trees to an open area. In 1.5 miles it delivers you to a beautiful lake at the base of Kavanaugh Ridge.

Back on Dunderberg Meadow Road, you begin a rapid descent, and eventually see the other end of Road 178, which courses up a beautiful valley. Soon you reach Green Lakes Road (142) **[N38°09.356' W119°13.043']** and, 3.4 miles farther, U.S. 395 **[N38°11.798' W119°13.142']**.

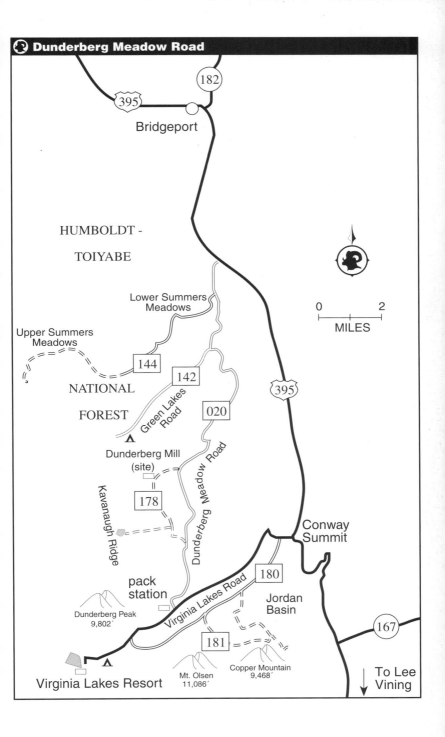

Ghost Town Loop

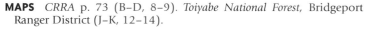

LOCATION In the Bodie Hills north of Mono Lake and east of Bridge-port (on U.S. 395). Mono County.

HIGHLIGHTS This beautiful high-desert drive takes you into the rolling Bodie Hills, which provide sweeping views of the Sierra Nevada and the Sweetwater Mountains to the west. It takes you through a historic mining district that includes the ghost towns of Masonic and, most notably, Bodie, California's best-preserved ghost town.

DIFFICULTY Easy.

TIME & DISTANCE 2–3 hours; 32 miles.

MAPS *CRRA* p. 73 (B–D, 8–9). *Toiyabe National Forest*, Bridgeport Ranger District (J–K, 12–14).

INFORMATION Humboldt-Toiyabe National Forest, Bridgeport Ranger District. BLM's Bishop Field Office. Bodie State Historic Park.

GETTING THERE In Bridgeport, take State Route 182 north for 3.8 miles from the junction with U.S. 395. Turn east onto Masonic Road (046) **[N38°18.555' W119°12.840']**. Set your odometer at 0. A remote but more interesting option is to take California S.R. 182 and Nevada State Route 338 north for 15 miles from Bridgeport, then turn east onto Sweetwater Road (028) **[N38°26.564' W119°07.886']**. In 1.8 miles turn south onto the northern leg of Masonic Road (046), and follow it for 6.7 miles into the hills to the site of Masonic, and continue the tour from there. This option, however, bypasses Chemung Mine and the spur to the summit of Masonic Mountain.

REST STOPS There are toilets and a picnic area at Bodie.

THE DRIVE After 5 miles the graded road reaches the ruins of Chemung Mine **[N38°20.989' W119°08.924']**, on the right, as you circle around 9,217-foot Masonic Mountain. This scenic stretch provides views of a range of features, particularly the Sierra Nevada and the Sweetwater Mountains, as it climbs to a saddle. At 7.7 miles from the highway is a 1.2-mile spur to the right that takes you up to an electronic site atop Masonic Mountain, where there's an outstanding 360-degree vista. From there the road descends to the junction with Bodie-Masonic Road (169) **[N38°21.273' W119°07.072']**, at the Upper Town section of bygone Masonic, a town spawned by a gold discovery in 1902. Masonic grew into three sections: Upper, Middle and Lower Town. The gold in these hills didn't follow any pattern, and finally ran out. Scavengers have hauled off most, but not all, of the town's remains over the years. Turn left (north) on Masonic Road (046) and drive through a canyon, and you soon reach the sites of Middle Masonic and Lower Town. There are a few ruins alongside the road, and old mines are still visible on the hillsides.

Return to the junction at Upper Town, and follow Road 169 east up a long draw, then south for almost 14 miles. You eventually round a turn and find yourself looking down on Bodie **[N38°12.769' W119°00.961']**, a raucous and short-lived gold-mining town that grew to 10,000 souls during its heyday (1879–1881). Today, it is maintained for posterity in a state that's been dubbed "arrested decay."

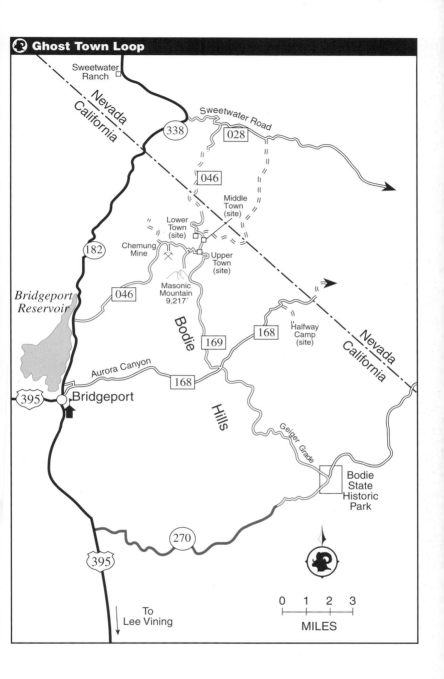

Sweetwater
Ranch

Nevada
California

Sweetwater Road

338

028

046

Middle
Town
(site)

Lower
Town
(site)

Chemung
Mine

Upper
Town
(site)

182

Masonic
Mountain
9,217´

046

Bodie

169

168

Halfway
Camp
(site)

Nevada
California

*Bridgeport
Reservoir*

Aurora Canyon

168

395

Bridgeport

Hills

Geiger Grade

Bodie
State
Historic
Park

270

395

To
Lee Vining

0   1   2   3

MILES

Ruins recall bygone times along the Ghost Town Loop (Tour 33).

Boulder Flat (Tour 34) lies high in the Sweetwater Mountains.

Boulder Flat

TOUR 34

LOCATION   In the Sweetwater Mountains. Humboldt-Toiyabe National Forest, 11 miles due north of Bridgeport (on U.S. 395). West of Nevada State Route 338 and the California/Nevada line. Mono County.

HIGHLIGHTS   The high-elevation views of the High Sierra from this beautiful neighboring range are magnificent. This route passes through an old gold- and silver-mining district where mountain peaks exceed 11,000 feet.

DIFFICULTY   Easy to moderate.

TIME & DISTANCE   2 hours and 18.2 miles round-trip to Boulder Flat. The additional routes described add another 1–2 hours and 5.4 miles.

MAPS   *CRRA* p. 73 (A–B, 7–8). *Toiyabe National Forest*, Bridgeport Ranger District (H–J, 12).

INFORMATION   Toiyabe National Forest, Bridgeport Ranger District.

GETTING THERE   From Bridgeport, drive north on State Route 182, which becomes Nevada State Route 338 at the state line. About 18.6 miles from the junction of U.S. 395 and S.R. 182, turn left (west) at Sweetwater Ranch onto Atchison Road (191) **[N38°28.279' W119°10.955']**. Zero the odometer.

REST STOPS   There are primitive campsites at Boulder Flat.

THE DRIVE   Keep to the left at the ranch, and drive slowly through it. At a fork at mile 1.1 drive through a gate, then turn left (south) onto Road 198 **[N38°27.578' W119°11.679']** where Road 191 continues toward the mountains. After several creek crossings there's a fork at mile 2.1 **[N38°26.470' W119°11.746']**, immediately after crossing a cattle guard (where the road crosses from Nevada into California). Road 198 goes right (west). Take it, and begin the rocky climb.

  At mile 4.9 make a hard right between pines **[N38°25.966' W119°13.169']**, then climb to a flat at mile 6.2, where the mining camp of Star City once stood **[N38°25.065' W119°14.638']**. Angle right, cross the flat, then go left at the wooden post. The mountainside road forks in 0.2 mile; keep left. A short distance farther, the route (Road 198) bends right (a two-track goes straight). The road becomes even rockier as it ascends toward a yellow-orange mountain. At mile 8.1 you emerge into pretty Boulder Flat, a basin and mining camp site at the base of 11,664-foot Wheeler Peak. Two log buildings of uncertain age and a number of foundations can be seen. The elevation here is about 10,300 feet.

  The road bends right (north) across Boulder Flat, passing among pines. It climbs to a vista point in a mile, and ends at inactive Frederick Mine just beyond that. Back at the log structures, where you first entered Boulder Flat, drive south through the trees, past another old log structure to a pond and a flat area. This is the vicinity of the bygone mining camp of Belfort **[N38°24.980' W119°16.024']**. The road descends via switchbacks to a gap where it follows Fryingpan Creek upstream to Long Meadow. There, turn left and cross the creek. The climb here (on Road 098) isn't difficult. At the top is a view of the Sierra from about 10,700 feet. Turn around here.

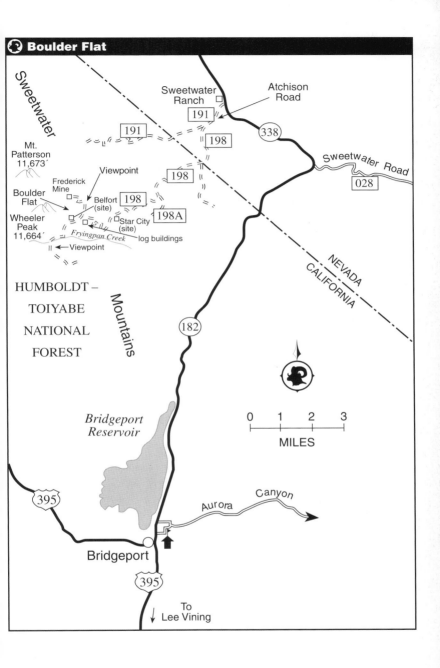

Sweetwater

Sweetwater
Ranch

Atchison
Road

191

191

198

338

Sweetwater Road

028

Mt.
Patterson
11,673'

Viewpoint

Frederick
Mine

Boulder
Flat

Belfort
(site)

198

198A

Wheeler
Peak
11,664'

Star City
(site)

198

Fryingpan Creek

log buildings

← Viewpoint

NEVADA

CALIFORNIA

HUMBOLDT –

TOIYABE

NATIONAL

FOREST

Mountains

182

*Bridgeport
Reservoir*

0   1   2   3

MILES

395

Aurora   Canyon

Bridgeport

395

To
↓ Lee Vining

TOUR 35

Jackass Flat

LOCATION Just west of the Nevada-California state line in Mono County; east of Walker and northwest of Bridgeport in the Sweetwater Mountains. Humboldt-Toiyabe National Forest. Mono County.

HIGHLIGHTS You will have spectacular views of the Sierra Nevada from a ridgeline drive high in the Sweetwater Mountains, a beautiful and accessible range east of the Sierra.

DIFFICULTY Easy to moderate.

TIME & DISTANCE 2.5 hours; 24.4 miles from U.S. 395 to Risue Road.

MAPS *CRRA* pp. 72–73 (A–B, 6–7) and 67 (H, 11–12). *Toiyabe National Forest,* Bridgeport Ranger District (G–H, 11–13).

INFORMATION Humboldt-Toiyabe National Forest, Bridgeport Ranger District.

GETTING THERE This north-south route can be taken in either direction. The scenery is great either way. **To go north (as described below):** From U.S. 395 about 14.6 miles northwest of Bridgeport, turn north onto Burcham (also spelled "Bircham," Tour 36) Flat Road (031) **[N38°21.197' W119°25.473']**. About 4.3 miles north of U.S. 395, turn east onto Road 067 **[N38°24.356' W119°25.167']** and follow it to Lobdell Lake (about 6.2 miles from Burcham Flat Road). At a Y junction at the southeast corner of the lake, set your odometer at 0 and go left **[N38°26.300' W119°21.743']**.

To go south: From U.S. 395 south of Topaz Lake, take Topaz Lane east to Eastside Road (3.5 miles). Follow Eastside Road north for about 1.8 miles to the junction with Risue Road. Then take Risue Road east 5.2 miles, then turn right (south) onto Road 195 and follow it south to Road 067.

REST STOPS Any place that's appealing.

THE DRIVE Going north, Road 067, the road you follow for most of this tour, runs along the west side of Lobdell Lake, then north of it. About 2.3 miles north of the Y junction at the southeast corner of the lake is another, smaller Y junction **[N38°27.989' W119°21.508']**. Go left (west). About 0.2 mile farther, at another small Y junction **[N38°28.018' W119°21.661']**, 067 angles right (north), up a hill, and climbs to a high, rocky and exposed ridge. Here you have terrific vistas of the Sierra and the Sweetwater Mountains. The latter include the three "sisters"—East Sister (10,402 feet), Middle Sister (10,859 feet) and South Sister (11,339 feet), as well as Mount Patterson (11,673 feet) and Wheeler Peak (11,664 feet). The two-track road of loose rock follows the ridge north. By mile 5.7 you descend steeply to a four-way junction **[N38°30.567' W119°21.201']**. Follow the road that goes north from the junction, along the west-facing mountain slope.

By about mile 7.4 you will be crossing broad Jackass Flat, where you may welcome the softer roadbed after so much rocky ridge-running. At mile 9.4 the road passes Jackass Spring **[N38°32.980' W119°22.363']**, marked by a corral. Another 0.4 mile after that is another junction **[N38°33.203' W119°22.083']**. Take the left (north) branch, Road 195. This easy road crosses the Nevada/California state line three times, bringing you to Risue Road, on the Nevada side, by mile 14 **[N38°35.831' W119°23.061']**. Go left (west), and drive 5.2 miles

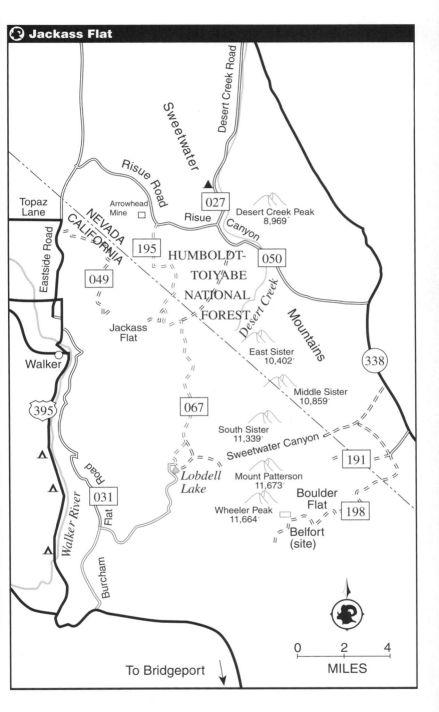

to Eastside Road **[N38°37.722' W119°26.977']**, then south into California and the town of Walker, on U.S. 395 **[N38°30.848' W119°27.452']**. Or go right and take the scenic Risue Road tour.

Burcham Flat Road

LOCATION Southwest of the Nevada line, in the Sweetwater Mountains just east of U.S. 395 and the Sierra. Humboldt-Toiyabe National Forest. This high north-south road parallels the Walker River and U.S. 395, between Walker and Fales Hot Springs. Mono County.

HIGHLIGHTS In January 1844 explorer Captain John C. Frémont, guide Kit Carson and a small band of half-starved men passed through these parts looking for the fabled Ventura River, which they thought would give them easy passage through the Sierra, to the west. They ended up forcing their way through the mountains in winter instead. You will enjoy outstanding mountain scenery on this alternative to U.S. 395, which road signs spell "Bircham" but which is spelled "Burcham" on most maps.

DIFFICULTY Easy. This is a maintained 2WD road, but the loose soil and gravel can make using high-range 4WD advisable if you start at the north end.

TIME & DISTANCE 45 minutes; 15 miles.

MAPS *CRRA* p. 72 (A–B, 6). *Toiyabe National Forest*, Bridgeport Ranger District (G, 11–13).

INFORMATION Humboldt-Toiyabe National Forest, Bridgeport Ranger District.

GETTING THERE This drive, which connects to U.S. 395 at both ends, can be driven north or south. The scenery is outstanding in both directions. **To drive south (as described below):** At the east end of Walker, on U.S. 395, turn north onto paved Eastside Road **[N38°30.848' W119°27.452']**. Almost 1.2 miles from the highway, turn right (east) onto paved Camp Antelope Road **[N38°31.705' W119°27.369']**. Go 0.2 mile, then veer right (southeast) onto unpaved Burcham Flat Road (031) **[N38°31.576' W119°27.130']**.

To go north: Take U.S. 395 north from Bridgeport for 14.6 miles. Turn right (north) onto Burcham (the sign spells it "Bircham") Flat Road. Set your odometer at 0.

REST STOPS Any place that appeals to you. Bridgeport is a pretty little town with all services.

THE DRIVE Going south from Walker, Burcham Flat Road climbs fairly steeply through semiarid canyons, taking you high above the canyon of the Walker River and U.S. 395. Soon the road angles into the mountains. After a few miles you have outstanding views, especially as the road takes you over a hill. Suddenly the Sierra loom ahead and to the west. Be sure to stop now and then and take in the equally dramatic alpine scenery behind you.

At mile 11.6 the road crosses a summit, at about 8,000 feet, and soon takes you past the turnoff to Lobdell Lake and Jackass Flat (Tour 35) **[N38°24.356' W119°25.167']**. Then comes the long, rapid descent on a manicured segment of road through Burcham Flat to U.S. 395 **[N38°21.197' W119°25.473']**. Watch your speed as you descend because it's easy to lose control on gravel.

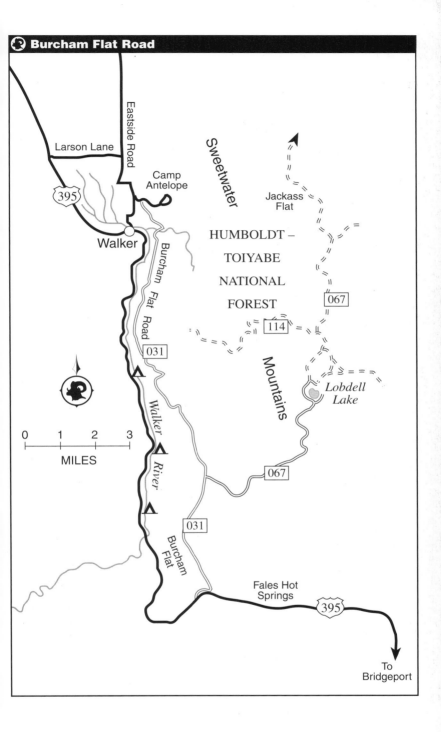

Eastside Road

Larson Lane

Camp Antelope

Sweetwater

Jackass Flat

395

Walker

HUMBOLDT –
TOIYABE
NATIONAL
FOREST

Burcham Flat Road

067

031

114

Mountains

Walker

Lobdell Lake

0   1   2   3
MILES

River

067

031

Burcham Flat

Fales Hot Springs

395

To Bridgeport

The California-Nevada line is marked on a boulder along the Jackass Flat tour (Tour 35), in the Sweetwater Mountains.

Burcham Flat Road (Tour 36) meanders through the Sweetwater Mountains high above the Walker River.

Risue Road

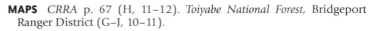

LOCATION In Douglas County, Nevada, just east of the state line in the Sweetwater Mountains of Humboldt-Toiyabe National Forest; northeast of Walker, California (on U.S. 395), in Mono County.

HIGHLIGHTS This tour of the semiarid desert that lies in the Sierra's rain shadow takes you along deep and very scenic Risue Canyon. It connects with the Jackass Flat drive (Tour 35).

DIFFICULTY Easy, although the western end of this maintained road can be very slick when wet.

TIME & DISTANCE 1 hour; about 16.5 miles.

MAPS *CRRA* p. 67 (H, 11–12). *Toiyabe National Forest,* Bridgeport Ranger District (G–J, 10–11).

INFORMATION Humboldt-Toiyabe National Forest, Bridgeport Ranger District.

GETTING THERE From Walker, on U.S. 395: Follow Eastside Road north for 8.4 miles. Turn right (east) at the well-marked turnoff for Risue Road (050) **[N38°37.722' W119°26.977']**. Set your odometer to 0.

From U.S. 395 south of Topaz Lake: Take Topaz Lane east to Eastside Road (3.5 miles). Take Eastside Road north for about 1.8 miles to the junction with Risue Road. Set your odometer to 0.

REST STOPS Stop along Desert Creek on the canyon floor, after you pass Desert Creek Road. You will see some primitive campsites.

THE DRIVE This fun and very scenic cruise takes you from about 5,460 feet to about 7,300 feet on a good dirt-and-gravel road. About 1.2 miles from Eastside Road you enter Risue Canyon, as you follow what will likely be a dry wash. By mile 2.8 it becomes a one-lane mountain road. Note the old Arrowhead Mine on the right at mile 4 **[N38°36.493' W119°23.714']**. At mile 5.2 is the road (195) to Jackass Flat **[N38°35.831' W119°23.061']**. As you continue to climb, by mile 6 you cross a summit, at about 7,300 feet. As the road descends it passes through much heavier vegetation, then follows the wall of a deep, rocky and wooded canyon.

At mile 7.9 is a turnout with a great view. A short distance farther is the turn north for Desert Creek Road (027) **[N38°35.746' W119°20.175']**. Stay on Risue Road, and the canyon floor soon becomes something of an oasis with some appealing, though undeveloped, campsites. After you climb out of the canyon, the undulating road delivers you to Nevada State Route 338.

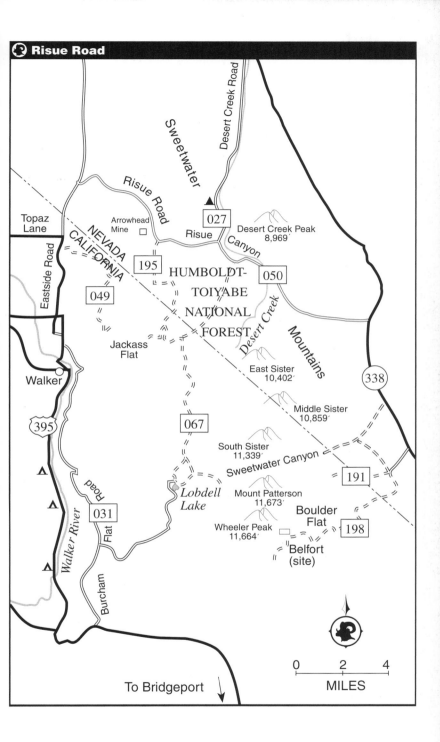

Sweetwater

Desert Creek Road

Risue Road

Topaz Lane

Arrowhead Mine

Risue Canyon

027

Desert Creek Peak 8,969'

NEVADA
CALIFORNIA

Eastside Road

195

HUMBOLDT-TOIYABE

049

050

Desert Creek

NATIONAL

Jackass Flat

FOREST

Mountains

East Sister 10,402'

Walker

395

338

067

Middle Sister 10,859'

South Sister 11,339'

Sweetwater Canyon

191

Road

031

Lobdell Lake

Mount Patterson 11,673'

Boulder Flat

198

Flat

Wheeler Peak 11,664'

Belfort (site)

Burcham

Walker River

0   2   4

MILES

To Bridgeport

Slickrock Trail

LOCATION South of State Route 4 at Lake Alpine. Stanislaus National Forest, at the west edge of the Carson-Iceberg Wilderness. Alpine County.

HIGHLIGHTS This isn't Moab, Utah's, famous mountain-biking trail. Instead, it's a short and beautiful 4WD trail to a granite outcropping where you can picnic in the shade beside lovely Silver Creek. Experienced four-wheelers can continue beyond the described route, on a challenging 4x4 trail to Utica Reservoir.

DIFFICULTY The narrow route is rocky in places, making high clearance and skid plates mandatory. I rate it moderately difficult as far as I take you. Beyond that, the Forest Service gives the 4x4 trail to Utica Reservoir a rating of very difficult.

TIME & DISTANCE From S.R. 4 it is 1.5 hours, depending on how much time you spend at Silver Creek; 3.6 miles round-trip.

MAPS *CRRA* p. 72 (A, 2). *Stanislaus National Forest* (B, 5).

INFORMATION Stanislaus National Forest, Calaveras Ranger District. Alpine Guard Station, near Bear Valley.

GETTING THERE Take S.R. 4 to the west end of Lake Alpine. Set your odometer at 0, then turn south onto the paved road to the Lake Alpine campground **[N38°28.684' W120°00.468']**. Just beyond the campground the road forks. The left branch is blocked, so you have to bear right on Road 7N01. The pavement ends 0.1 mile from the highway.

REST STOPS Silver Creek. There are developed campgrounds in the vicinity of Lake Alpine; refer to your map. Primitive camping along this route is allowed after the first 0.7 mile.

THE DRIVE Watch for potholes as you wind through pine forest, on what is still an easily traveled road along the lake's southwestern shore. A half mile from the highway, angle right (a private driveway is on the left), and the road diminishes to a narrow, single-lane track through the forest. It's necessary to go slowly as you maneuver between trees and over roadbed rocks, so this might be a good time to shift into low-range for better low-speed control.

At about mile 1.5 the trail (and "trail" describes it accurately), brings you to gorgeous Silver Creek. There is a substantial rock ledge to get over here. From now on the stream cascades through the surface granite in many places, but none is more idyllic than the oasis you reach at mile 1.8 **[N38°27.405' W120°00.248']**. You can park here among the pines. If you want to consider continuing on to Utica Reservoir, first walk a short distance farther down the trail and inspect a rocky, gnarly granite crack that you'll have to crawl through.

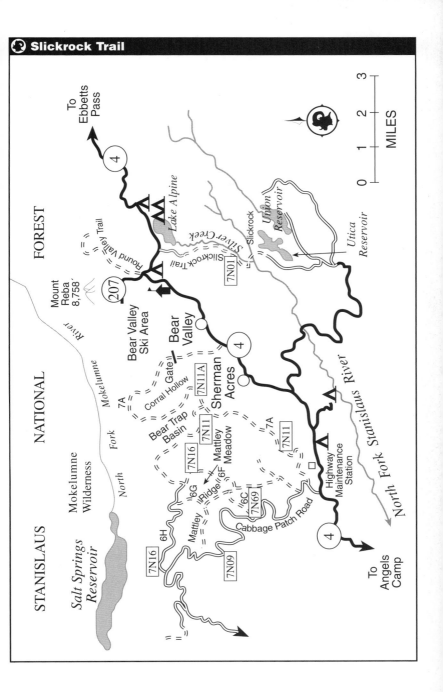

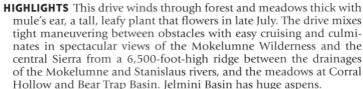

Bear Trap
and Corral Hollow

LOCATION Stanislaus National Forest. North of State Route 4 and west of Bear Valley and Lake Alpine. Alpine County.

HIGHLIGHTS This drive winds through forest and meadows thick with mule's ear, a tall, leafy plant that flowers in late July. The drive mixes tight maneuvering between obstacles with easy cruising and culminates in spectacular views of the Mokelumne Wilderness and the central Sierra from a 6,500-foot-high ridge between the drainages of the Mokelumne and Stanislaus rivers, and the meadows at Corral Hollow and Bear Trap Basin. Jelmini Basin has huge aspens.

DIFFICULTY The eastern leg, Route 7A from S.R. 4 near Bear Valley to Bear Trap Basin is moderate to difficult. The Corral Hollow trail (7N11 and 7N11A) between Cabbage Patch Road (7N09) and Bear Trap Basin, is easy. Be prepared to maneuver between trees and rocks, and to remove deadfall from the roadway.

TIME & DISTANCE 3 hours; 14 miles.

MAPS *CRRA* p. 72 (A–B, 1–2). *Stanislaus National Forest* (B, 4–5). Also get a copy of the Calaveras Ranger District's off-highway vehicle route map.

INFORMATION Stanislaus National Forest, Calaveras Ranger District.

GETTING THERE This loop can be taken in either direction. **To evaluate the rougher segment early on:** Begin on Route 7A at S.R. 4 **[N38°27.405' W120°03.164']**, about 0.6 mile west of Bear Valley. Look for a small sign with a 4WD symbol on the north side of the highway, and a CORRAL HOLLOW OHV route sign. Zero your odometer there.

To go in the opposite direction: About 6.8 miles southwest of Bear Valley turn north from S.R. 4 onto Cabbage Patch Road (7N09). In 0.9 mile turn right at the sign for Road 7N11 to Corral Hollow.

REST STOPS Old Bear Trap cabin, in Bear Trap Basin, is a pleasant place. It also has the only toilet on the route.

THE DRIVE Route 7A is a slow, narrow, rutted, rocky but pretty forest trail that passes or crosses a number of meadows. There is a steep and loose uphill section at mile 1.8, but at mile 2.3 you are amply rewarded for your effort when you reach a ridge overlooking the canyon of the North Fork of the Mokelumne River, and the Mokelumne Wilderness. (You're also next to Bear Valley's ski runs.) The route angles left (west) here **[N38°28.757' W120°03.823']**, climbing high along the ridge to a spectacular viewpoint at mile 3. Then the road descends southward through the meadow of Corral Hollow.

At mile 3.8 is a chewed-up spot, but it shouldn't be a problem. By mile 5.2 you enter a picturesque meadow, Bear Trap Basin, where you see Bear Trap Cabin, an old cowboy cabin now owned by the Forest Service. The road south is much better. It climbs out of the basin and makes a long, scenic descent to the southwest via Roads 7N11A and 7N11.

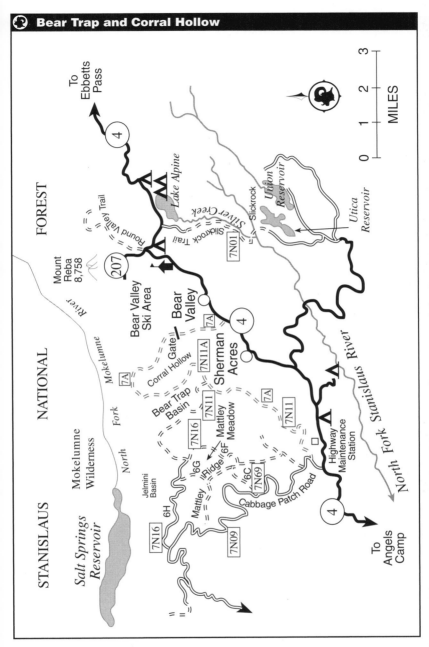

At mile 1.8 from Bear Trap Basin, 4WD Road 7N11 spurs to the right (northwest) **[N38°27.672' W120°05.347']**, to Jelmini Basin, where the aspens are remarkably large. Continuing south, you reach Cabbage Patch Road (7N09) in 4.7 miles **[N38°25.602' W120°07.274']**. Turn left there, and soon you will be at S.R. 4 **[N38°24.766' W120°08.168']** once more.

The tour to Corral Hollow winds through picturesque forest.

Bear Trap Cabin, in Bear Trap Basin, is an old cowboy cabin.

Round Valley Trail

LOCATION North of State Route 4 at Lake Alpine. Stanislaus National Forest. Alpine County.

HIGHLIGHTS This is a convenient, short but exhilarating 4WD road that climbs steeply to a summit about 8,842 feet high, with spectacular vistas across the Sierra and into the canyons and valleys of the Mokelumne Wilderness. It ends at the wilderness boundary, at the Lake Valley Trailhead of the unofficial, but nonetheless popular, Tahoe-Yosemite Trail.

DIFFICULTY Moderate. The road is steep, rocky and chewed up in places.

TIME & DISTANCE 45 minutes; 5.3 miles round-trip.

MAPS *CRRA* p. 72 (A, 2). *Stanislaus National Forest* (A–B, 5), and the Calaveras Ranger District's off-highway vehicle trail brochure.

INFORMATION Stanislaus National Forest, Calaveras Ranger District. The Alpine Guard Station, at Bear Valley.

GETTING THERE Just 0.1 mile west of Silvertip Campground, west of Lake Alpine, turn north from State Route 4 onto State Route 207 toward the Bear Valley Ski Area. At 0.1 mile from S.R. 4, look for a dirt road on the right (east) side of the road marked by a 4WD symbol (typically a simple jeep symbol) and an orange arrow **[N38°29.086' W120°01.181']**. That is the route. Zero your odometer there.

REST STOPS The summit is a great place to spend time. Lake Alpine has many amenities, including campgrounds.

THE DRIVE This road used to be the Mt. Reba Trail because it went up to a former lookout on Mt. Reba, which is about a mile west of where the road ends. Now, the road ends at a summit about a mile from Mt. Reba. The road winds steeply through forest and across open hillsides above the east end of Round Valley, providing magnificent high-elevation views of the glacial valleys, lakes, canyons, and granite domes and spires of the Sierra. At mile 2.2 from S.R. 207 is a fork **[N38°30.411' W120°00.619']**; keep left. You reach the summit 2.7 miles from S.R. 207 **[N38°30.411' W120°00.619']**.

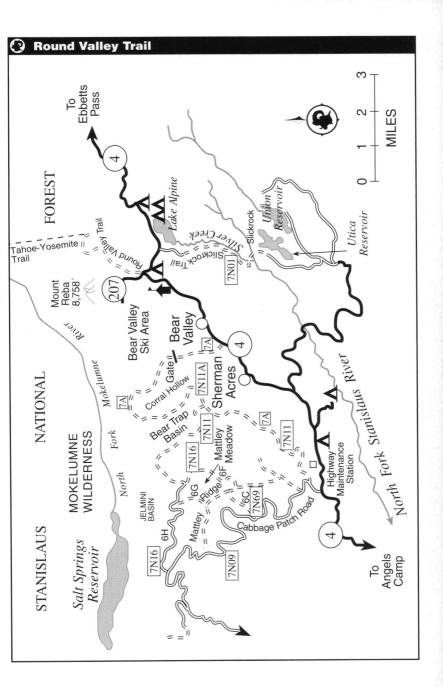

Mattley Ridge Loop

LOCATION Stanislaus National Forest. North of State Route 4 and west of Bear Valley and Lake Alpine. Alpine County.

HIGHLIGHTS This rather unique Sierra drive mixes moderate four-wheeling with easy cruising through a range of landscapes, from forest to Mattley Meadow, where the trail passes through areas thick with a large leafy plant commonly called mule's ear, which usually flowers in late July. It also provides outstanding high-elevation vistas across the canyons, valleys and peaks of the rugged Mokelumne Wilderness.

DIFFICULTY Moderate to difficult, with some maneuvering between narrowly spaced trees and rocks. Be prepared to either remove or maneuver around deadfall in the roadway.

TIME & DISTANCE 1.5 hours; 8.6 miles. There are variations and other worthwhile routes to explore in the area.

MAPS *CRRA* p. 72 (A, 1). *Stanislaus National Forest* (B, 4–5). Also get a copy of the Calaveras Ranger District's off-highway vehicle route map.

INFORMATION Stanislaus National Forest, Calaveras Ranger District.

GETTING THERE At 6.8 miles southwest of Bear Valley turn north from S.R. 4 onto Cabbage Patch Road (7N09) **[N38°24.766' W120°08.168']**. Take Cabbage Patch Road north 3.9 miles, then turn right (northeast) onto Road 7N69 (Off-Highway Vehicle Trail 6C) **[N38°26.537' W120°08.787']**. Zero your odometer.

REST STOPS Bear Valley has food and fuel. There are many developed campgrounds in the area; refer to your map.

THE DRIVE Like many roads and trails in this area, Road 7N69 is a designated off-highway vehicle route with an additional numeric designation (6C) on the Calaveras District's OHV route map. Watch for signs with those designations. You will also see yellow arrows denoting OHV routes. This one climbs up to Mattley Ridge. At mile 1, on the ridge, you reach a junction; OHV Route 6A is to the left and right **[N38°27.124' W120°08.027']**. This is the Mattley Ridge Loop, a designated OHV route that you will follow but will eventually depart from. Bear right here. In a half mile take a narrow, rudimentary 4WD road (6F) **[N38°26.922' W120°07.859']** that angles to the left and descends down the north side of the ridge to sprawling and lush Mattley Meadow. The road follows the perimeter of the meadow, then enters it at mile 2.6 amid stands of unusually large aspens. Here the narrow road passes through a meadow thick with leafy mule's ear, providing a unique Sierra driving experience.

At mile 3.9 is a much better road, 7N16 (6H) **[N38°28.397' W120°07.583']**. Just before you reach it, you have to make a very tight maneuver between a boulder and a tree. Bear left (west) on 7N16. In 1.5 miles OHV Route 6G branches to the left **[N38°28.420' W120°08.358']** to climb back up to Mattley Ridge via one particularly nasty spot and complete the loop where you began this drive. However, I recommend continuing west on 7N16, which provides great views of the canyon of the North Fork of the Mokelumne River and the Mokelumne Wilderness before taking you back to Cabbage Patch Road in 4.7 miles **[N38°28.581' W120°10.497']**.

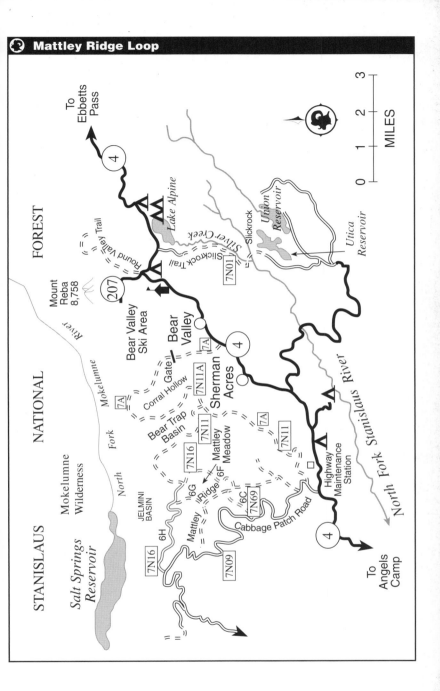

Leviathan Peak Loop

LOCATION Just north of State Route 89 at Monitor Pass. Humboldt-Toiyabe National Forest. Alpine County.

HIGHLIGHTS You will find outstanding views from the crest of the Sierra, especially if you take the short side trip to the nearby summit of Leviathan Peak (8,963 feet), site of an electronics site and Leviathan Lookout, built in 1957 and the last one in Humboldt-Toiyabe National Forest. The route is good for mountain biking as well.

DIFFICULTY Easy.

TIME & DISTANCE 1.5 hours; 5.3 miles. This tour can be taken in either direction.

GETTING THERE From the junction of S.R. 89 and State Route 4 south of Markleeville, drive east on S.R. 89 for 7.6 miles to Monitor Pass **[N38°40.537' W119°37.247']**. Or from U.S. 395 south of Topaz Lake, take S.R. 89 west for 8 miles to Monitor Pass. In a large meadow just west of a roadside historical marker on the pass, turn north from S.R. 89 onto Road 083, a two-track to the right of two ponds **[N38°40.232' W119°37.632']**. Drive toward a saddle with a rocky peak on the left and a rock outcrop on the right. Reset your odometer to 0 at the highway.

MAPS CRRA p. 67 (G, 10). *Toiyabe National Forest,* Carson Ranger District (E–F, 10).

INFORMATION Humboldt-Toiyabe National Forest, Carson Ranger District.

REST STOPS Any place that appeals to you.

THE DRIVE You're going to circle around the base of Leviathan Peak, which offers a fantastic 360-degree panorama from Leviathan Lookout, built in 1957, at the summit. At about mile 0.6 there's a spur to the left, which goes a short distance to a ridge with views of the valley to the west. Soon the main road veers east, at nearly 8,400 feet, giving you fine vistas of Nevada's desert ranges.

At 1.8 miles from the highway you pass through a large aspen grove, which promises a spectacular display of color in early autumn. When you reach mile 3.4, there is a rocky downhill pitch. Mile 3.6 should find you at a fork **[N38°41.529' W119°36.143']**; go straight. At mile 3.8 the road takes you past Big Spring, to your left, as you head south toward the highway. A quarter mile farther take a track to the left **[N38°41.259' W119°35.751']** a short distance to Indian Springs Road (085, Tour 43). Turn right when you reach it, toward the highway, just a half mile away **[N38°40.860' W119°35.623']**.

To go up Leviathan Peak, from S.R. 89 just east of the Monitor Pass historical marker take the short drive up Leviathan Lookout Road (057) **[N38°40.485' W119°36.940']**. Partway up park at a locked gate, then walk about a quarter mile to the lookout tower on the summit **[N38°41.033' W119°36.720']**. The incredible vista there makes it worth every step.

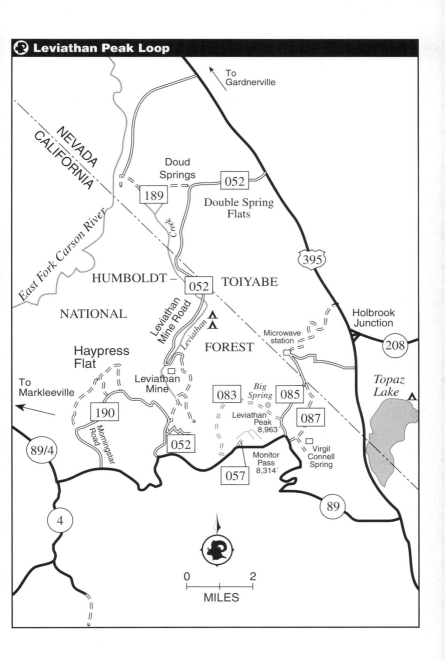

To
Gardnerville

NEVADA
CALIFORNIA

Doud
Springs

052

189

Double Spring
Flats

Creek

395

East Fork Carson River

HUMBOLDT – 052 TOIYABE

NATIONAL

Leviathan Mine Road

Leviathan

FOREST

Microwave
station

Holbrook
Junction

208

Haypress
Flat

Leviathan
Mine

083

Big
Spring

085

Topaz
Lake

To
Markleeville

190

Morningstar Road

Leviathan
Peak
8,963

087

052

Virgil
Connell
Spring

89/4

Monitor
Pass
8,314

057

89

4

0   2
MILES

Monitor Pass to U.S. 395

LOCATION This tour follows Indian Springs Road (a.k.a. Road 085) down from Monitor Pass on State Route 89 to U.S. 395 in Nevada, just north of Topaz Lake. Humboldt-Toiyabe National Forest. Alpine County.

HIGHLIGHTS This exhilarating 2,600-foot descent from Monitor Pass to U.S. 395, on a mountainside road has an outstanding view east into the Great Basin. The highly scenic alternate via Road 087 and Virgil Connell Spring is worth exploring as well.

DIFFICULTY Easy, but there are long drop-offs that some might find unsettling.

TIME & DISTANCE An hour; 7 miles.

MAPS *CRRA* p. 67 (G, 10). *Toiyabe National Forest*, Carson Ranger District (F, 10).

INFORMATION Humboldt-Toiyabe National Forest, Carson Ranger District.

GETTING THERE **From the junction of S.R. 89 and State Route 4 south of Markleeville:** Take S.R. 89 east almost 10 miles to Monitor Pass.

　　From U.S. 395: Take S.R. 89 west a little more than 7 miles to Monitor Pass. Turn north onto Indian Springs Road (085) **[N38°40.860' W119°35.623']**. Set your odometer at 0.

REST STOPS It's a short drive, so just stop at appropriate places to enjoy the view.

THE DRIVE From S.R. 89, Indian Springs Road is a good dirt and gravel backcountry route. You will pass 8,963-foot Leviathan Peak, to your left; you can drive to within a short distance of the top, where the view from Leviathan Lookout, built in 1957 and the last one in Humboldt-Toiyabe National Forest, is even more incredible. At mile 2.7, as you pass through rolling hills of sagebrush and grass, the road crosses the Nevada line. You'll see an electronics site ahead; drive toward it, and turn right when you get there. Now you will have a great view of Carson Valley, far below.

　　At mile 3.5 there's a fork to the left **[N38°43.273' W119°35.283']**; go straight, staying on the gravel road. The view is absolutely magnificent at this point, as you wind down the mountainside on what becomes a good single-lane road. Eventually the road levels out and comes out at U.S. 395 **[N38°42.904' W119°33.214']** north of Topaz Lake.

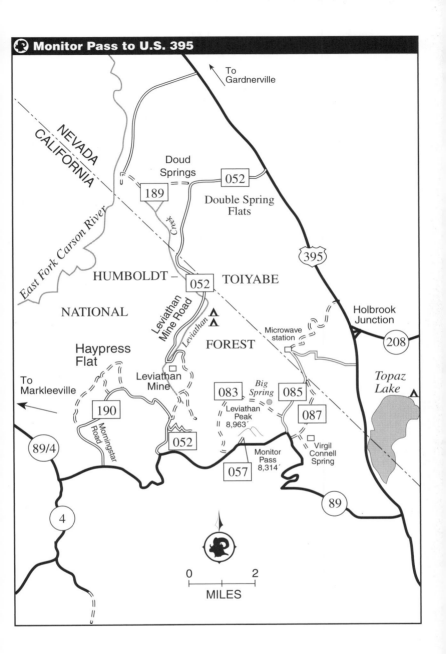

To
Gardnerville

NEVADA
CALIFORNIA

Doud
Springs

052

189

Double Spring
Flats

395

East Fork Carson River

Creek

HUMBOLDT – 052 TOIYABE

NATIONAL

Leviathan Mine Road

Leviathan

Microwave
station

Holbrook
Junction

208

Haypress
Flat

Leviathan
Mine

FOREST

083   Big
Spring   085

Topaz
Lake

To
Markleeville

190

083   Big
Spring   085

087

Morningstar Road

052

Leviathan
Peak
8,963´

Virgil
Connell
Spring

89/4

057

Monitor
Pass
8,314´

4

89

0   2
MILES

The going gets a bit rough at this spot on the Leviathan Peak Loop (Tour 42).

The Monitor Pass tour (Tour 43) provides outstanding vistas as it descends to U.S. 395.

Haypress Flat Loop

LOCATION North of State Route 89; east of Markleeville. Humboldt-Toiyabe National Forest. Alpine County.

HIGHLIGHTS Road 190, a.k.a. Morningstar Road, and the side road to Haypress Flat will take you through a beautiful corner of the Sierra where the superlative scenery includes the High Sierra, meadows and canyons. Stands of aspen make it a fine late summer or early autumn drive. There is quite a network of optional, and sometimes rough, 4WD spurs to explore as well. The mines in this old mining district add interest, but require caution. This tour can be linked with Leviathan Mine Road (Tour 45).

DIFFICULTY Easy overall, but spurs can be much more difficult.

TIME & DISTANCE 1.5 hours; 9.4 miles.

MAPS *CRRA* p. 67 (G, 9–10). *Toiyabe National Forest*, Carson Ranger District (E, 10).

INFORMATION Carson Ranger District. Markleeville Guard Station, in Markleeville.

GETTING THERE About 1.7 miles east of the intersection of S.R. 89 and State Route 4 south of Markleeville, turn north from S.R. 89 onto Road 190, Morningstar Road **[N38°39.948' W119°41.878']**. Set your odometer at 0.

REST STOPS While there are no developed stopping places, there are some primitive campsites and scenic places to stop.

THE DRIVE At the turnoff from S.R. 4, where you will see large tailings piles, is the site of the vanished town of Monitor (later called Loope), a center for silver, copper and some gold mining from the late 1850s to the late 1890s. The road climbs steeply but easily up Loope Canyon. At mile 1 you're at the top of the canyon, where Road 190 angles right **[N38°40.661' W119°42.488']**. At mile 1.5 Road 190 bends sharply to the right, and you see a pullout and a good primitive campsite on the left with a great view down into Mogul Canyon.

At mile 1.8 Road 190B branches left (north) **[N38°41.027' W119°42.611']**. (You can continue on Road 190 for a shorter but still very worthwhile version of this tour.) Road 190B takes you on a scenic loop of about 3.2 miles, through pretty Haypress Flat and then south to rejoin Road 190 only 1.5 miles northeast of this point **[N38°41.927' W119°41.717']**. Or, instead of taking 190B south to rejoin 190, drive a bit farther north and east across Haypress Flat, and take Road 056 **[N38°42.793' W119°41.351']** south to rejoin Road 190. Back on 190, you descend through conifers and aspen stands, get a peek at Leviathan Mine and come out on Leviathan Mine Road (052) **[N38°41.250' W119°39.529']**. You can turn left (north), past Leviathan Mine to U.S. 395, on the route of Tour 45. Or to complete this tour, go right (south) to reach S.R. 89 in 1.5 miles **[N38°40.153' W119°39.974']**.

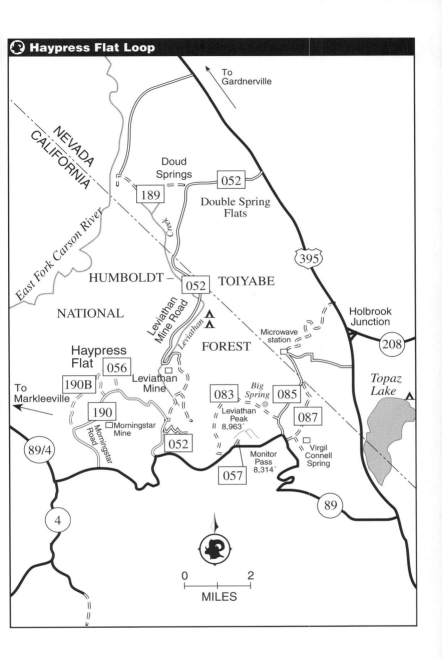

Leviathan Mine Road

LOCATION Near the California-Nevada line, between California State Route 89 west of Monitor Pass and U.S. 395. Humboldt-Toiyabe National Forest. Alpine County.

HIGHLIGHTS The inactive Leviathan open-pit sulfur mine, proposed in 1999 for mitigation under the federal Superfund program, and the acid mine drainage that has sterilized streams and threatened the East Fork Carson River are a shocking anomaly in an otherwise beautiful area. This drive takes you through forests, canyons and high-desert mountains, and past the mine itself. It can be linked with Haypress Flat (Tour 44).

DIFFICULTY Easy, on a maintained dirt-and-gravel road. Be careful on the blind curves.

TIME & DISTANCE 1 hour; 15 miles.

MAPS *CRRA* p. 67 (F–G, 10). *Toiyabe National Forest*, Carson Ranger District (E–F, 9–10).

INFORMATION Toiyabe National Forest, Carson Ranger District. Markleeville Guard Station.

GETTING THERE From S.R. 89 (as described below): From the junction of S.R. 89 and State Route 4 south of Markleeville, take S.R. 89 east for 4.7 miles. Turn left (north) onto Leviathan Mine Road (Road 052) **[N38°40.153' W119°39.974']**. Or take S.R. 89 west from U.S. 395 for about 12 miles, then turn right (west) onto Leviathan Mine Road.

From U.S. 395: Leviathan Mine Road (052) is 9.9 miles south of the traffic light at Pinenut Road, at the south end of Gardnerville, Nevada. Set your odometer to 0.

REST STOPS There are a number of places to stop for views of the region, particularly where the road is high above the mine. There are some primitive campsites at various spots along Leviathan Creek north of the mine.

THE DRIVE Leviathan Mine Road is a good dirt-and-gravel county road in the high country of the Sierra's eastern slope. At mile 1.5 is the left (west) turn for Morningstar Road (190) and Haypress Flat **[N38°41.250' W119°39.529']**. Almost a mile farther, angle right where a sign warns that the road is not suited for passenger cars.

From here you come upon places that provide a bird's-eye view of Leviathan Mine, an inactive sulfur mine dating back to 1863, when extracted copper sulfate was used for processing silver ore in Nevada's Comstock Lode. The off-and-on mining that occurred there afterward ended in 1962, but the environmental devastation has continued. About 22 million tons of overburden and waste rock were dumped into and along the channels of Leviathan and Aspen creeks when the mine was active. Water seepage into and through the pit and huge tailings piles create acidic drainage that flows into Leviathan Creek. Today, Leviathan and Bryant creeks are devoid of aquatic life, and fish kills have occurred in the East Fork of the Carson River, 10 miles downstream.

Beyond the mine you drive along beautiful Leviathan Canyon, cross the Nevada line **[N38°45.749' W119°39.383']** and then head east across Double Spring Flat to U.S. 395 south of Gardnerville.

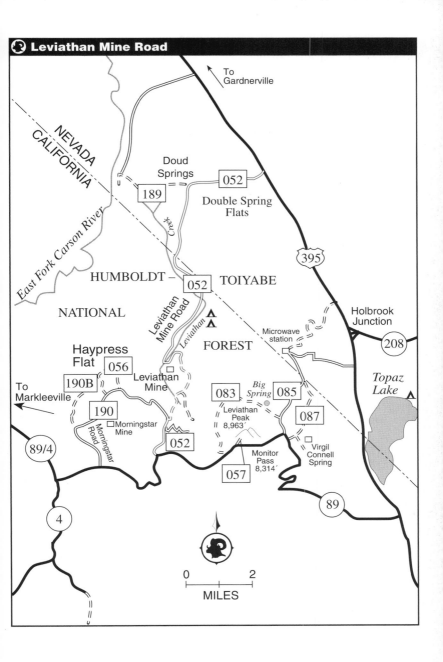

NEVADA
CALIFORNIA

To
Gardnerville

Doud
Springs

052

189

Double Spring
Flats

Creek

East Fork Carson River

395

HUMBOLDT – 052 TOIYABE

NATIONAL

Leviathan Mine Road

Leviathan

Holbrook
Junction

FOREST

208

Microwave
station

Topaz
Lake

Haypress
Flat

056

190B

083 Big 085
Spring

Leviathan
Mine

Leviathan
Peak
8,963'

087

190

Morningstar
Mine

Virgil
Connell
Spring

Monitor
Pass
8,314'

89/4

Morningstar Road

052

057

To
Markleeville

4

89

0   2
MILES

A roadside barrel along Leviathan Mine Road marks the California-Nevada border.

Acid-mine drainage from Leviathan Mine has left streams sterile.

Blue Lakes and Indian Valley

LOCATION Eldorado National Forest, south of State Route 88 and Carson Pass, at the edge of the Mokelumne Wilderness. Alpine County.

HIGHLIGHTS There are many beautiful lakes and meadows, as well as vistas of the Mokelumne Wilderness. There also are opportunities for hiking, camping, fishing and mountain biking.

DIFFICULTY Forestdale Road (a.k.a. Forestdale Creek Road) and Blue Lakes Road are easy. Blue Lakes Road is paved for 6 miles south of S.R. 88, then it's maintained gravel for the next 6 miles or so to Lower Blue Lake (this segment is expected to be paved eventually). About 3 miles south of Red Lake, Forestdale Road becomes a narrow shelf road that can be blocked by slow-melting snow well into summer. The roads in the Little Indian Valley and Indian Valley areas are easy to moderate.

TIME & DISTANCE 1.5–2 hours and 20 miles for the loop around Blue Lakes alone. The segment to Indian Valley adds 8 to 10 miles and another 1 to 1.5 hours.

MAPS *CRRA* p. 67 (G–H, 7–8). *Eldorado National Forest* (J, 4–6).

INFORMATION Eldorado National Forest, Amador Ranger District.

GETTING THERE This loop can be taken in either direction, beginning or ending at S.R. 88. The description below begins just east of Carson Pass. From S.R. 88 at the eastern end of Red Lake, take the Red Lake turnoff south onto Forestdale Creek Road (013) **[N38°41.945' W119°57.956']**, then the left fork through a large green gate. Set your odometer at 0 there.

REST STOPS Lost Lakes and Forestdale Divide are pretty. There are developed campgrounds at Upper and Lower Blue Lakes and at Hope Valley near S.R. 88 and established primitive camping areas in the Indian Valley area as well.

THE DRIVE At 1.5 miles Forestdale Road crosses a bridge over Forestdale Creek. You'll see signs for Lost Lakes and Upper Blue Lake. A short distance farther is a fork **[N38°40.696' W119°57.604']**; keep right. The road climbs, becoming a single lane at mile 1.9. By mile 3 you're at a point where I've found the road blocked by snow as late as August. Just beyond there is Forestdale Divide **[N38°39.669' W119°58.001']**, where the road and the Pacific Crest Trail intersect in a subalpine setting at about 8,800 feet. Descend from there toward Upper and Lower Blue Lakes, but take the spur to pretty Lost Lakes **[N38°38.889' W119°57.100']**. (There is an optional spur later on **[N38°36.570' W119°55.446']**, via Road 9N01 to Twin and Meadow lakes that is worth exploring as well.)

There are fairly steep stretches beyond the Lost Lakes turnoff as you drive through forest to Upper Blue Lake. At the southern tip of Lower Blue Lake, turn east and then north on Blue Lakes Road (015), a busy road in summer that follows the West Fork Carson River to reach S.R. 88 in about 12 miles (the latter half of the road is paved) **[N38°45.080' W119°56.522']**. After a mile turn right (southeast) onto Sunset Lake Road (097) **[N38°37.165' W119°54.644']**, and follow it to Indian

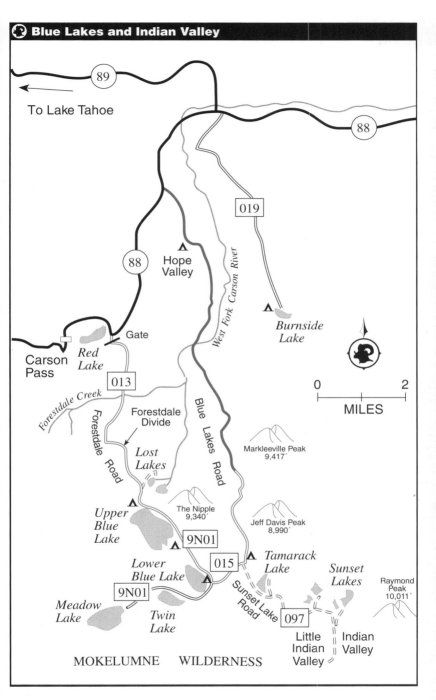

Blue Lakes and Indian Valley

To Lake Tahoe

89

88

019

88

Hope
Valley

West Fork Carson River

Burnside
Lake

Gate

Carson
Pass

Red
Lake

013

Forestdale Creek

Forestdale
Divide

Forestdale Road

Lost
Lakes

Blue Lakes Road

Markleeville Peak
9,417´

0   2
MILES

The Nipple
9,340´

Upper
Blue
Lake

Jeff Davis Peak
8,990´

9N01

015

Tamarack
Lake

Sunset
Lakes

Raymond
Peak
10,011´

Lower
Blue Lake

9N01

Sunset Lake Road

097

Meadow
Lake

Twin
Lake

Little
Indian
Valley

Indian
Valley

MOKELUMNE   WILDERNESS

Valley and Little Indian Valley, where there is a network of small roads (with stream crossings) to several lakes. After you've explored these areas, turn around and continue to the highway on Blue Lakes Road.

Genoa Peak Road

LOCATION This tour is on the Nevada side of the Lake Tahoe Basin. It extends between U.S. 50 at the north end (just south of Spooner Junction) and Nevada State Route 207 at Daggett Pass at the south end. The road follows the crest of the Carson Range, at the east edge of the Lake Tahoe Basin Management Unit (LTBMU). Douglas County, Nevada.

HIGHLIGHTS This high (over 8,000 feet much of the way) mountain road provides great views of the Lake Tahoe Basin, especially from the 9,150-foot summit of Genoa Peak. Along the northern segment, Logan House Road, a side route just west of Genoa Peak Road, is a pretty alternative to Genoa Peak Road.

DIFFICULTY Easy.

TIME & DISTANCE 2 hours; 10.2 miles for Genoa Peak Road, including the Genoa Peak spur (1 mile round-trip). Logan House Road is 6.5 miles but omits a portion of Genoa Peak Road.

MAPS CRRA p. 67 (D, 8). *Lake Tahoe Basin Management Unit* (C, 4–5).

INFORMATION LTBMU. Lake Tahoe Visitors Center.

GETTING THERE You can take this north-south drive in either direction. **To go north (as described below):** From the junction of U.S. 50 and Nevada State Route 207, on the lake's southeastern shore, take S.R. 207 east for 2.8 miles, up the Kingsbury Grade toward Daggett Pass. Turn left (north) onto North Benjamin Drive **[N38°58.537' W119°53.650']**, which becomes Andria Drive. About 1.7 miles from S.R. 207 is the nonmotorized Tahoe Rim Trail trailhead **[N38°59.687' W119°53.777']**. Set your odometer at 0 here. Genoa Peak Road (14N32) is directly ahead.

   To go south: From Glenbrook, take U.S. 50 east toward Spooner Junction, at Ponderosa Ranch Road. Just before the junction, turn right (east) off the highway and drive around behind the Nevada Department of Transportation's Spooner maintenance station, where Genoa Peak Road begins. Logan House Road (14N33) is 1.5 miles from U.S. 50, on the right **[N39°05.086' W119°53.590']**.

REST STOPS Genoa Peak.

THE DRIVE At the south end, Genoa Peak Road used to be an eroding maze of dirt tracks. In addition to erosion control efforts, the Forest Service has obliterated the many confusing spurs, and now the route is easy to follow.

   About 1.3 miles north of the Tahoe Rim Trail trailhead, the road crosses a small basin. Go straight, over a hump. At about mile 3.5 is the left (west) turn for Logan House Road (14N33 on the signposts; 14N24 on the map). Look for a white designated route marker. It's a pleasant drive through aspen stands, meadows and conifer forest strewn with granite. Despite having logged areas, it's a prettier alternative to the bypassed section of Genoa Peak Road. (It rejoins Genoa Peak Road in 6.5 miles **[N39°05.086' W119°53.590']**.)

   About 0.8 mile north of this southern junction with Logan House Road is the right (east) turn to Genoa Peak, where you'll find a 360-degree panorama of the Lake Tahoe Basin and, to the east,

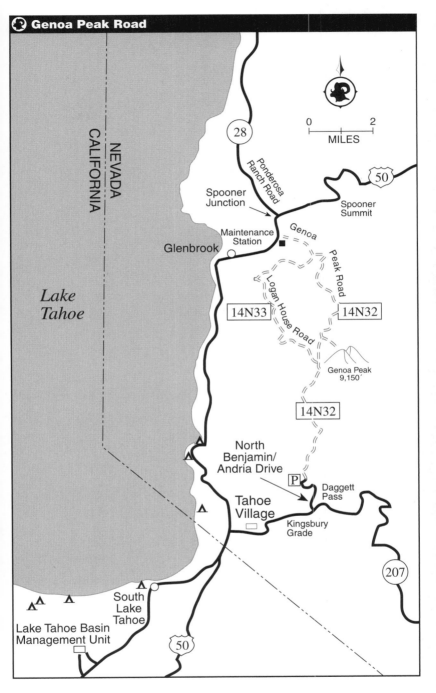

Carson Valley. (One option is to go up to Genoa Peak, then backtrack to Logan House Road.) After a steady, easy descent Genoa Peak Road delivers you to U.S. 50 at the Nevada Department of Transportation's Spooner maintenance station **[N39°05.896' W119°54.617']**.

Indian Valley (Tour 46) is known for its broad meadows.

Genoa Peak (Tour 47) provides a view across Lake Tahoe.

Barker Pass Loop

LOCATION In the Forest Service's Lake Tahoe Basin Management Unit (LTBMU). On the west side of Lake Tahoe, and west of State Route 89 and McKinney Bay. It links the lakeside communities of Tahoma and Idlewild. Placer County.

HIGHLIGHTS Pretty lakes and streams, waterfowl and mountain vistas are among the attractions of this convenient backroad outing.

DIFFICULTY Easy to moderate, with road conditions ranging from asphalt to graded dirt, loose rock and possibly large mud holes.

TIME & DISTANCE About 2.5 hours; 19 miles.

MAPS *CRRA* p. 66 (C–D, 5–6). *Lake Tahoe Basin Management Unit* (C, 2).

INFORMATION LTBMU. Lake Tahoe Visitors Center.

GETTING THERE You can take this loop from two points on S.R. 89 on Lake Tahoe's west shore. **From Tahoma:** Going this direction allows you to appraise the toughest section early. Turn southwest off S.R. 89 onto paved McKinney-Rubicon Springs Road **[N39°04.218' W120°08.409']** and follow the signs for Miller Lake. Cross Evergreen Way, and follow the OHV (off-highway vehicle) signs to the McKinney-Rubicon OHV Staging Area. The pavement ends there. Continue on Road 3013.

From Idlewild: Turn west from S.R. 89 onto paved Blackwood Canyon/Barker Pass Road (Road 3). In 2.2 miles, where the road bends left to cross Blackwood Creek, continue ahead on graveled Road 15N38 through the Blackwood Canyon OHV Staging Area. Follow 15N38 (moderate) along Middle Fork Blackwood Creek to Barker Pass Road (3.8 miles). Go right (west) there and drive 1.3 miles, then turn left (south) onto Road 3013.

REST STOPS There are toilets at the OHV staging areas, primitive campsites at Miller, Richardson and Bear lakes, and a developed campground at Kaspian.

THE DRIVE Beyond the asphalt at the McKinney-Rubicon OHV staging area, the road (3013) is rocky, loose and steep. Along the way you may see serious four-wheelers heading to or returning from the famously difficult Rubicon Trail, an arduous 4WD trail that is for expert four-wheelers.

About 2 miles from the OHV area is McKinney Lake, where you may encounter a series of large and deep mud holes that you'll need to maneuver around. Then the road passes Lily Lake **[N39°02.353' W120°11.408']** and, beyond that, Miller Lake, where you might see waterfowl. (There's more solitude at Richardson Lake, an easy mile up a left turn **[N39°02.093' W120°12.284']** just beyond Miller Lake.) About 1.2 miles from Miller Lake, across from a parking area and near a bridge, is the turnoff for the Rubicon Trail **[N39°02.232' W120°13.341']**. Follow the main road through the gate here, and climb north past pretty Bear Lake. About 5 miles from Bear Lake is a T intersection **[N39°04.529' W120°15.343']**. Turn right to reach Barker Pass in about 1.3 miles **[N39°04.593' W120°14.147']**. It's about a half mile from the summit to pavement and another 6.9 miles to the highway **[N39°06.804' W120°09.478']**.

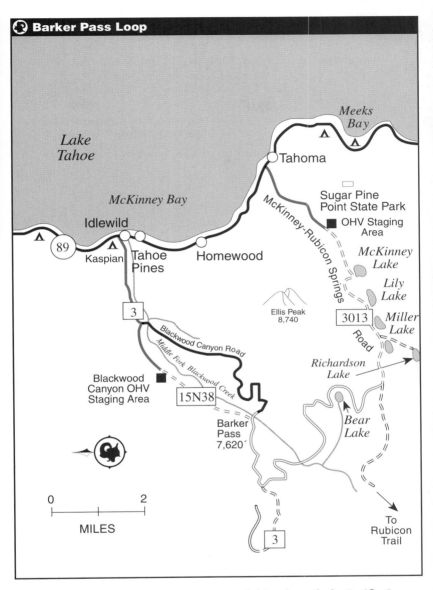

For more fun and scenery, turn into and drive through the Pacific Crest Trail parking area and take the 4WD road (15N38) along Middle Fork Blackwood Creek. Road 15N38 connects to Blackwood Canyon Road **[N39°06.388' W120°11.803']** 2.2 miles west of S.R. 89.

Mount Watson

LOCATION West of Lake Tahoe, between State Route 89 and State Route 267 and southwest of Brockway Summit on S.R. 267. In the Forest Service's Lake Tahoe Basin Management Unit (LTBMU). Placer County.

HIGHLIGHTS The 8,424-foot summit of Mt. Watson provides a view of Lake Tahoe, with more views of the Sierra on the way down.

DIFFICULTY Easy to moderate, on former logging roads.

TIME & DISTANCE 1.5–2 hours; 16.4 miles round-trip from Brockway Summit, on S.R. 267.

MAPS *CRRA* pp. 66–67 (B–C, 6–7). *Lake Tahoe Basin Management Unit* (A–B, 2–3).

INFORMATION LTBMU. Lake Tahoe Visitors Center.

GETTING THERE **From Lake Tahoe's north shore (as described below):** Take S.R. 267 (North Shore Boulevard) about 3.2 miles northwest to Brockway Summit. Zero your odometer.
   From Truckee: Take S.R. 267 (Brockway Road) southeast to Brockway Summit. At Brockway Summit turn west onto Mt. Watson Road (73) **[N39°15.634' W120°04.284']**. Set your odometer to 0. As you can see on the map, Road 06 (easy) also will get you from Truckee to Mt. Watson (12 miles).

REST STOPS Watson Lake and the summit of Mt. Watson.

THE DRIVE For the first 4 miles you are on a graveled Forest Service road. At mile 5.9 you will see road 16N73C on the left **[N39°13.778' W120°08.739']**. It goes 0.7 mile to Watson Lake. From this turnoff, it's about 0.7 mile farther to Road 73M, a fairly steep two-track that angles sharply to the left **[N39°13.502' W120°08.917']**. This is the road to the summit of Mt. Watson. It's about 1.6 miles from here to the summit **[N39°13.206' W120°08.834']**, along a shelf, and the view from the top, amid tall pines and granite boulders, is absolutely magnificent. The views on the return drive are good as well.

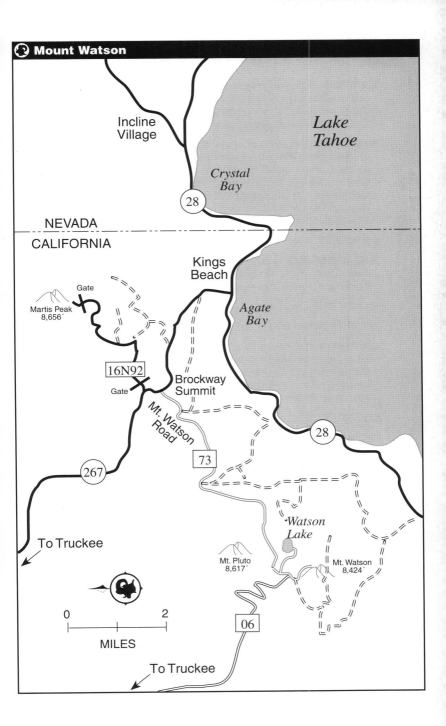

Incline
Village

*Lake
Tahoe*

*Crystal
Bay*

28

NEVADA

CALIFORNIA

Kings
Beach

*Agate
Bay*

Gate

Martis Peak
8,656´

16N92

Gate

Mt. Watson
Road

Brockway
Summit

73

28

267

Watson
Lake

To Truckee

Mt. Pluto
8,617´

Mt. Watson
8,424´

0   2

MILES

06

To Truckee

Martis Peak

LOCATION At the northwestern edge of the Forest Service's Lake Tahoe Basin Management Unit (LTBMU), and 4 miles due north of Kings Beach on Lake Tahoe's north shore, and about 1.5 miles west of the California-Nevada line. Placer County.

HIGHLIGHTS Stunning views of the Tahoe Basin and surrounding region from the historic, visitor-friendly Martis Peak fire lookout, built in 1914. It was deactivated in the late 1970s, and vandals did a great deal of damage in the mid-1990s. It was subsequently restored by volunteers, the California Department of Forestry and Fire Protection, and Tahoe National Forest. It is staffed five days a week. Friendly volunteers will greet you on weekends. A gate is locked at 6 PM.

DIFFICULTY Easy, on a crudely paved Forest Service road.

TIME & DISTANCE About 1.5 hours; 8 miles round-trip from State Route 267 (a.k.a. Brockway Road from Truckee, and North Shore Boulevard from Kings Beach).

MAPS CRRA p. 67 (B, 7). *Lake Tahoe Basin Management Unit* (A, 3).

INFORMATION LTBMU. Lake Tahoe Visitors Center.

GETTING THERE Take S.R. 267 about 3.2 miles northwest from Kings Beach over Brockway Summit, or about 8.5 miles southeast from Truckee toward Brockway Summit. About 0.4 mile north of the summit, take the first eastbound road (Martis Peak Road, 16N92) **[N39°16.027' W120°04.473']**, along Martis Creek. Set your odometer to 0.

REST STOPS The summit of Martis Peak.

THE DRIVE After turning up Martis Creek, drive 1.9 miles to a junction **[N39°16.634' W120°03.025']**, then continue on Road 16N92.

At mile 2.6 is another intersection **[N39°17.004' W120°02.524']**. Continue straight. At almost mile 3.3 is a fork **[N39°16.995' W120°01.958']**. A rough trail, No. 92B, goes straight, but you don't want that. Bear left (the road may not have a sign). About a half mile farther the road becomes steeper. Vistas appear, and soon you can see the old fire lookout **[N39°17.534' W120°02.079']**. Drive up to it and park. Climb up to the lookout and take in an amazing sight. You're at 8,656 feet on the lookout. Lake Tahoe, at 6,229 feet, is more than 2,000 feet below.

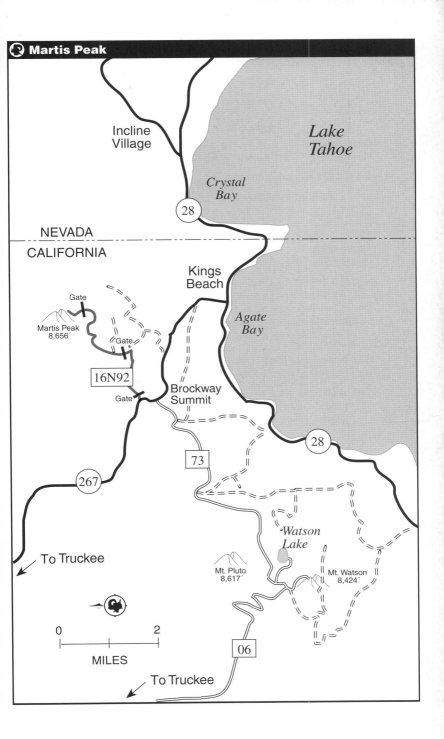

Incline Village

Lake Tahoe

Crystal Bay

28

NEVADA

CALIFORNIA

Kings Beach

Agate Bay

Gate

Martis Peak 8,656'

Gate

16N92

Gate

Brockway Summit

28

73

267

Watson Lake

Mt. Pluto 8,617'

Mt. Watson 8,424'

To Truckee

0   2

MILES

06

To Truckee

Crystal Peak Loop

LOCATION Humboldt-Toiyabe National Forest, just west of the California-Nevada state line about 5 miles northwest of Verdi, Nevada, which is just off Interstate 80 about 10 miles west of Reno. Sierra County.

HIGHLIGHTS This convenient and highly scenic tour provides vistas across Dog Valley to Reno and into the Great Basin.

DIFFICULTY Easy, but the roadbed is rocky in places.

TIME & DISTANCE 1.5 hours; 20 miles starting and ending in Verdi.

MAPS *CRRA* p. 61 (G, 9–10). *Toiyabe National Forest,* Carson Ranger District (B, 3).

INFORMATION Humboldt-Toiyabe National Forest, Carson Ranger District.

GETTING THERE In Verdi, zero your odometer at the junction of U.S. 40 (the main street) and Bridge Street, then take Bridge Street northwest toward Dog Valley-Henness Pass Road. Go past the elementary school and cross two bridges. Immediately after the second bridge turn right, onto Dog Valley-Henness Pass Road (Tour 4), and follow it through a residential area. At mile 0.9 you cross from Nevada into California. Continue toward Dog Valley. The pavement ends at mile 1.5, in the national forest.

REST STOPS Crystal Peak Park along the Truckee River, at the west end of Verdi, is a lovely place to have a picnic. Dog Valley Campground has shade, tables and pit toilets, but no potable water.

THE DRIVE Road 002, Dog Valley-Henness Pass Road, climbs gradually up a ravine lined with pines, some of them charred by wildfires. At mile 3.9 is a fork **[N39°32.945' W120°02.388']**. Take the right branch (Long Valley Road, still 002), and soon you begin descending into the bowl of Dog Valley. The road passes the Dog Valley Guard Station at mile 5.4 **[N39°33.596' W120°03.205']**. At mile 5.8 turn left onto Road 038 **[N39°33.898' W120°03.315']**, which soon becomes crystalline-white in color.

You reach another junction at mile 6.3 **[N39°33.760' W120°03.789']**, where the spur (038) to Dog Valley Campground branches right. Take Road 073 directly ahead (there may be a small sign for the Crystal Peak Loop). It becomes a narrow shelf that takes you up the west wall of Dog Valley just below 8,103-foot Crystal Peak, eventually switchbacking higher and providing fabulous views east across the valley to Reno and into the desert beyond. (Across the valley looms Peavine Peak. Consulting your map, you will see that you can drive across the valley and make a great loop around the base of the peak, and even up to it.) After following the shelf north, you switchback down to reconnect with Road 038. Go left, again passing Dog Valley Campground, and retrace your route to Verdi.

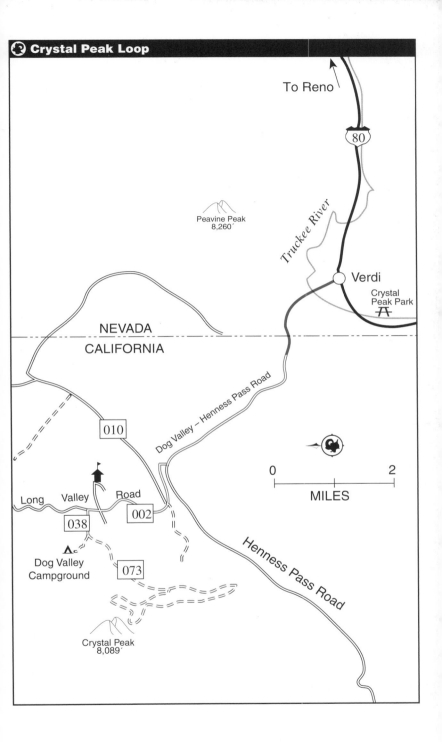

To Reno

80

Truckee River

Peavine Peak
8,260′

Verdi

Crystal
Peak Park

NEVADA

CALIFORNIA

Dog Valley – Henness Pass Road

010

Long   Valley   Road

002

038

Dog Valley
Campground

073

Henness Pass Road

Crystal Peak
8,089′

0   2

MILES

Sand Canyon Road (Tour 25) leads toward the John Muir Wilderness above Rock Creek Canyon.

Tours by Theme

These particular attractions can be found along the tour specified by name. The tour number is provided in parentheses.

Easy Access

Iowa Hill Loop (6)
Just off Interstate 80 less than 50 miles northeast of Sacramento.

Alabama Hills (17)
A fascinating and beautiful side trip off U.S. 395 at the base of the Sierra near the town of Independence.

Buttermilk Country (23)
A spectacular and famous climbing area near Bishop, on U.S. 395.

Horse Meadows Loop (30)
Just south of Lee Vining (on U.S. 395), the eastern gateway to Yosemite.

Copper Mountain Loop (31)
Immediately west of U.S. 395 at Conway Summit.

Dunderberg Meadow Road (32)
Easy and very pretty, it can be linked with Copper Mountain Loop (Tour 31) if you're traveling on U.S. 395 south of Bridgeport.

Burcham Flat Road (36)
A historic alternative to U.S. 395 south of Walker with sweeping views of the Sierra.

Crystal Peak Loop (51)
An ideal morning or afternoon drive a few miles west of Reno, Nevada.

Ecological Transitions

Jawbone to Lake Isabella (13)
The transition zone between the Mojave Desert, noted for its Joshua trees, and the piney forests of the rugged southern Sierra is fascinating and beautiful.

The Narrows and Papoose Flat (20)
At the western edge of the Great Basin, the steep, rugged but accessible Inyo Mountains stand in the semiarid rain shadow of the Sierra Nevada, which saps moisture from the Pacific air currents.

Silver Canyon and the White Mountains (21)
Nearly as high as the heavily forested Sierra Nevada—the highest mountain range in the Lower 48—the semiarid and sparsely wooded White Mountains could hardly be more different from their rivals a few miles to the west. The Sierra rain shadow leaves the highest range in the Great Basin with little moisture from Pacific air currents. So the Whites never experienced the glaciation that carved the Sierra. Despite the harsh, dry climate, ancient bristlecone pines that live for thousands of years thrive here.

Buttermilk Country (23)
Driving along the base of the Sierra Nevada's dramatic eastern escarpment is to experience the very meeting place of the semiarid Great Basin and one of the snowiest places on Earth.

Volcanic Tableland (24)
Formed by both volcanic and glacial forces, the high-desert valleys that lie in the rain shadow of the Sierra Nevada—vales like Owens Valley and Mono Basin—are genuine lands of fire and ice.

Four-Wheeling

Wheeler Ridge Road (26)
Substantial rock outcrops make this the most challenging trail in the book, and one of the most rewarding.

Historic Sites

Diggins I (2)
A 4WD adventure deep in the heart of the mother lode.

Diggins II (3)
Explore rugged and remote gold-rush country that few ever see.

Henness Pass Road (4)
The last trans-Sierra dirt road has served dreamers since the gold rush.

Iowa Hill Loop (6)
The beautiful canyons and mountainsides are still recovering from 19th-century hydraulic mining.

Ghost Town Loop (33)
Backroads take you through bygone mining camps and into Bodie State Historic Park, one of the West's best-preserved gold-mining ghost towns.

Burcham Flat Road (36)
In 1844, explorer Captain John C. Frémont, guide Kit Carson and a band of half-starved men passed this way searching for the fabled Ventura River.

Vistas

Sierra Buttes Loop (1)
This 4WD adventure provides awesome views of the historic North Yuba River Valley and the northern Sierra, particularly after the hike to the lookout atop 8,587-foot Sierra Buttes.

Black Rock Road (8)
A high, heart-pounding shelf road provides views deep into the canyon of the North Fork of the Kings River.

Armstrong Canyon (18)
A narrow old mining road snakes up the dramatic escarpment of the eastern Sierra.

Inyo Mountains (19)
Standing in the rain shadow of the Sierra Nevada, the Inyo Mountains form the eastern wall of the 10,000-foot-deep Owens Valley. From their peaks and crest, the Inyos—especially Mazourka Peak—offer dramatic north-south views of the High Sierra and the semiarid Great Basin.

Coyote Flat and Coyote Ridge (22)
Another old mining road takes you high above Owens Valley to lofty heights with some of the High Sierra's most inspiring sights.

Buttermilk Country (23)
Lying at the base of the soaring eastern Sierra, the spectacular area known as "the Buttermilks" has long been popular in the sport of bouldering.

Sand Canyon Road (25)
A small, rocky road high above hectic Rock Creek Canyon takes you well above the crowds while providing some of the region's most beautiful alpine views.

Wheeler Ridge Road (26)
A 4WD road that is challenging but doable in some stock SUVs (e.g., 4Runners and Land Cruisers) leads to a dramatic overlook and primitive camping site thousands of feet above Owens Valley.

Laurel Canyon (27)
Just outside Mammoth Lakes, a rocky little road follows a stunning glacial canyon to a group of beautiful subalpine lakes.

San Joaquin Ridge (29)
Although short, this 4WD road at Mammoth Lakes is among the eastern Sierra's most exhilarating and beautiful.

Copper Mountain Loop (31)
Particularly beautiful in late summer and early autumn, when the aspens turn golden, this loop lets you gaze far out across the moonscape of the volcanic Mono Basin as well as along the spine of the Sierra Nevada.

Jackass Flat (35)
Although the Sweetwater Mountains, which stand east of the Sierra, aren't well known, this beautiful and accessible range offers multihued peaks that exceed 11,000 feet, excellent views of the long spine of the Sierra and outstanding high-elevation primitive camping.

Round Valley Trail (40)
An exhilarating 4WD trail climbs steeply to a summit over 8,800 feet high that provides views across the Sierra and into the canyons and valleys of the Mokelumne Wilderness.

Monitor Pass to U.S. 395 (43)
The 2,600-foot descent from Monitor Pass to U.S. 395 involves a mountainside road with outstanding views into the Great Basin.

Genoa Peak Road (47)
At elevations over 8,000 feet much of the way, this mountain road gives you a bird's-eye view of the Lake Tahoe Basin, especially from the summit of 9,150-foot Genoa Peak.

Contact Information

4X4NOW.com and 4X4BOOKS.com
Books, maps, advice, articles, etc.

Automobile Club of Southern California (ACSC)
3350 Harbour Boulevard
Costa Mesa, CA 92626
(714) 427-5950
www.aaa.com

Bodie State Historic Park
P.O. Box 515
Bridgeport, CA 93517
(760) 647-6445
www.parks.ca.gov

Bureau of Land Management
www.blm.gov/ca/caso/

Bakersfield Field Office
3801 Pegasus Drive
Bakersfield, CA 93308
(661) 391-6000
www.blm.gov/ca/bakersfield

Bishop Field Office
351 Pacu Lane, Suite 100
Bishop, CA 93514
(760) 872-5000
www.blm.gov/ca/bishop

California State Office
2800 Cottage Way, Suite W-1834
Sacramento, CA 95825
(916) 978-4400
www.blm.gov/ca/caso/

Jawbone Station
28111 Jawbone Canyon Road
Cantil, CA 93519
(760) 373-1146
E-mail: jawbone@ccis.com

California Association of 4WD Clubs
8120 36th Avenue
Sacramento, CA 95824
(916) 381-8300
www.cal4wheel.com

California Campground Reservation System
(800) 444-PARK

California State Automobile Association
150 Van Ness Avenue
San Francisco, CA 94102
(415) 565-2141
www.csaa.com

Eldorado National Forest
www.fs.fed.us/r5/eldorado/

Information Center
100 Forni Road
Placerville, CA 95667
(530) 644-6048

Amador Ranger District
26820 Silver Drive
Pioneer, CA 95666
(209) 295-4251

Eastern Sierra Interpretive Association
798 North Main Street
Bishop, CA 93514
(619) 873-2500

Humboldt-Toiyabe National Forest
www.fs.fed.us/r4/htnf

Supervisor's Office
1200 Franklin Way
Sparks, NV 89431
(775) 331-6444

Bridgeport Ranger District
HC 62 Box 1000
Bridgeport, CA 93517
(760) 932-7070

Carson Ranger District
1536 South Carson St.
Carson City, NV 89701
(775) 882-2766

Inyo National Forest
351 Pacu Lane, Suite 200
Bishop, CA 93514
(760) 873-2400
www.fs.fed.us/r5/inyo

Ancient Bristlecone Pine Visitors Center
White Mountains' Schulman Grove
(760) 873-2500 (recorded info.)
Open only in summer

**Eastern Sierra Interagency
Visitors Center**
Intersection of State Routes 395
and 136
P.O. Drawer R
Lone Pine, CA 93545
(760) 876-6222

**Mammoth Lakes Ranger Station
and Visitors Center**
P.O. Box 148
Mammoth Lakes, CA 93546
(760) 924-5500

**Mono Basin Scenic Area
Visitors Center**
U.S. 395 just north of
Lee Vining
P.O. Box 429
Lee Vining, CA 93541
(760) 647-3044

Mount Whitney Ranger Station
P.O. Box 8 or 640 South Main St.
Lone Pine, CA 93545
 (760) 876-6200

White Mountain Ranger Station
798 North Main Street
Bishop, CA 93514
(760) 873-2500

Lake Tahoe Basin Management Unit
U.S. Forest Service
35 College Drive
South Lake Tahoe, CA 96150
(530) 543-2600
Visitors Center: (530) 573-2674
www.fs.fed.us/r5/ltbmu

Malakoff Diggins State Historic Park
23579 North Bloomfield Park Road
Nevada City, CA 95959
(530) 265-2740
www.parks.ca.gov

**Mono Lake Committee Information
Center and Bookstore**
U.S. 395 at Third Street or
P.O. Box 29
Lee Vining, CA 93541
(760) 647-6595
www.monolake.org

National Park Reservation System
(800) 365-2267
http://reservations.nps.gov

**Placer County Public Works
Department**
(530) 745-7500
www.placer.ca.gov

Plumas National Forest
159 Lawrence Street or
P.O. Box 11500
Quincy, CA 95971
(530) 283-2050
www.fs.fed.us/r5/plumas

Feather River Ranger District
875 Mitchell Avenue
Oroville, CA 95965
(530) 534-6500

Sequoia National Forest
www.fs.fed.us/r5/sequoia

Supervisor's Office
1839 South Newcomb Street
Porterville, CA 93257
(559) 784-1500

Kernville River Ranger District

Kernville Office
P.O. Box 9
Kernville, CA 93238
(760) 376-3781

Lake Isabella Office
4875 Ponderosa Drive or
P.O. Box 3810
Lake Isabella, CA 93240
(760) 379-5646

Hume Lake Ranger District
35860 East Kings Canyon Road
Dunlap, CA 93621
(559) 338-2251

Sierra National Forest
1600 Tollhouse Road
Clovis, CA 93612
(559) 297-0706
www.fs.fed.us/r5/sierra

High Sierra Ranger District
29688 Auberry Road
P.O. Box 559
Prather, CA 93651
(559) 855-5355

Stanislaus National Forest
19777 Greenley Road
Sonora, CA 95370
(209) 532-3671
www.fs.fed.us/r5/stanislaus

Calaveras Ranger District
P.O. Box 500
Hathaway Pines, CA 95233
(209) 795-1381

Tahoe National Forest
631 Coyote Street
Nevada City, CA 95959
(530) 265-4531
www.fs.fed.us/r5/tahoe

American River Ranger District
22830 Foresthill Road
Foresthill, CA 95631
(530) 367-2224

Big Bend Visitors Center
49685 Hampshire Rocks Road
(Interstate 80 at Big Bend-
Rainbow Road exit)
P.O. Box 830
Soda Springs, CA 95631
(530) 426-3609

Sierraville Ranger District
317 South Lincoln Street
P.O. Box 95
Sierraville, CA 96126
(530) 994-3401

Truckee Ranger District
9646 Donner Pass Road
Truckee, CA 96161
(530) 587-3558

Yuba River Ranger District
15924 Highway 49
Camptonville, CA 95922
(530) 288-3231

Tulare County Transportation Branch
(559) 733-6291
www.co.tulare.ca.us

References

Browning, Peter. *Place Names of the Sierra Nevada.* Berkeley, CA: Wilderness Press, 1991.

Heizer, R. F., and Whipple, M. A. *The California Indians: A Source Book.* Berkeley, CA: University of California Press, 1972.

Hill, Mary. *Geology of the Sierra Nevada.* Berkeley, CA: University of California Press, 2006.

Hill, Russell B. *California Mountain Ranges.* Helena, MO; Falcon Press, 1986.

Holliday, J. S. *The World Rushed In: The California Gold Rush Experience.* Norman, OK; University of Oklahoma Press, 2002.

Irwin, Sue. *California's Eastern Sierra: A Visitor's Guide.* Los Olivos, CA: Cachuma Press, 1992.

McPhee, John. *Assembling California.* New York City: Farrar, Straus and Giroux, 1994.

Mitchell, Roger. *Eastern Sierra Jeep Trails.* Glendale, CA: La Siesta Press, 1992.

——. *Inyo Mono Jeep Trails.* Glendale, CA: La Siesta Press, 1991.

——. *Western Sierra Jeep Trails.* Glendale, CA: La Siesta Press, 1983.

Nadeau, Remi. *Ghost Towns and Mining Camps of California: A History and Guide.* Santa Barbara, CA: Crest Publishers, 1998.

Olmsted, Gerald W. *The Best of the Sierra Nevada.* New York City: Crown Publishers, Inc., 1991.

Schoenherr, Allan A. *A Natural History of California.* Berkeley, CA: University of California Press, 1995.

INDEX

Note: Page references in **bold** indicate a tour;
page references in *italics* indicate a photograph.